DATE DUE

JUL 2 3 2005			
JUL 2 0 2007			
DGS 12-4-07			
APR 1 6 2008			
DEC 0 1 2009			
FEB 0 1 2011			

Demco, Inc. 38-293

WOMEN IN NORTH AMERICA'S RELIGIOUS WORLD

WOMEN'S ISSUES:
GLOBAL TRENDS

Women in the Arab World

Women in the World of Japan

Women in the World of Africa

Women in the World of China

Native Women in the Americas

Women in the World of India

Women in the Eastern European World

Women in the World of Southeast Asia

Women in the Hispanic World

Women in the World of Russia

Women in the Mediterranean World

Women in North America's Religious World

WOMEN'S ISSUES:
GLOBAL TRENDS

WOMEN IN NORTH AMERICA'S RELIGIOUS WORLD

BY
KENNETH R. MCINTOSH

Mason Crest Publishers
Philadelphia

Mason Crest Publishers Inc.
370 Reed Road
Broomall, Pennsylvania 19008
(866) MCP-BOOK (toll free)

First printing.
1 2 3 4 5 6 7 8 9 10
ISBN 1-59084-868-3
ISBN 1-59804-856-X (series)

Library of Congress Cataloging-in-Publication Data

McIntosh, Kenneth, 1959-
  Women in North America's religious world / by Kenneth R. McIntosh.
    p. cm. — (Women's issues, global trends)
  Includes bibliographical references and index.
  ISBN 1-59084-868-3
  1. Women and religion—North America. I. Title. II. Series.

  BL458.M4 2005
  200'.82'0973—dc22
                              2004002817

Interior design by Michelle Bouch and MK Bassett-Harvey.
Illustrations by Michelle Bouch.
Produced by Harding House Publishing Service, Inc.
Cover design by Benjamin Stewart.
Printed in India.

CONTENTS

Introduction • 7

Author's Preface • 11

ONE

Women in North American Catholicism • 15

TWO

Women in North America's Evangelical Churches • 27

THREE

Women in the Mormon Church • 35

FOUR

Amish and Mennonite Women • 45

FIVE

Women in African American Christianity • 55

SIX

Women in North American Judaism • 67

SEVEN

North American Muslim Women • 77

EIGHT

North American Buddhist Women • 87

NINE

North American Hindu Women • 97

TEN

North American Women Who Practice
Wicca and Neopaganism • 107

Further Reading • 117

For More Information • 119

Glossary • 121

Index • 124

Picture Credits • 127

Biographies • 128

INTRODUCTION

by Mary Jo Dudley

The last thirty years have been a time of great progress for women around the world. In some countries, especially where women have more access to education and work opportunities, the relationships between women and men have changed radically. The boundaries between men's roles and women's roles have been crossed, and women are enjoying many experiences that were denied them in past centuries.

But there is still much to be done. On the global stage, women are increasingly the ones who suffer most from poverty. At the same time that they produce 75 to 90 percent of the world's food crops, they are also responsible for taking care of their households. According to the United Nations, in no country in the world do men come anywhere near to spending as much time on housework as women do. This means that women's job opportunities are often extremely limited, contributing to the "feminization of poverty."

In fact, two out of every three poor adults are women. According to the Decade of Women, "Women do two-thirds of the world's work, receive 10 percent of the world's income, and own one percent of the means of production."

Women often have no choice but to take jobs that lack long-term security or adequate pay; many women work in dangerous working conditions or in unprotected home-based industries. This series clearly illustrates how historic events and contemporary trends (such as war, conflicts, and migration) have also contributed to women's loss of property and diminished access to resources.

A recent report from Human Rights Watch indicates that many countries continue to deny women basic legal protections. Amnesty International points out, "Governments are not living up to their promises under the Women's Convention to protect women from discrimination and violence such as rape and female genital mutilation." Many nations—including the United States—have not ratified the United Nations' Women's Treaty.

During times of armed conflict, especially under policies of ethnic cleansing, women are particularly at risk. Murder, torture, systematic rape, forced pregnancy, and forced abortions are all too common human rights violations endured by women around the world. This series presents the experience of women in Vietnam, Cambodia, the Middle East, and other war-torn regions.

In the political arena, equality between men and women has still not been achieved. Around the world, women are underrepresented in their local and national governments; on average, women represent only 10 percent of all legislators worldwide. This series provides excellent examples of key female leaders who have promoted women's rights and occupied unique leadership positions, despite historical contexts that would normally have shut them out from political and social prominence.

The Fourth World Conference on Women called upon the international community to take action in the following areas of concern:

• the persistent and increasing burden of poverty on women
• inequalities and inadequacies in access to education and training

- inequalities and inadequacies in access to health care and related services
- violence against women
- the effects of armed or other kinds of conflict on women
- inequality in economic structures and policies, in all forms of productive processes, and in access to resources
- insufficient mechanisms at all levels to promote the advancement of women
- lack of protection of women's human rights
- stereotyping of women and inequality in women's participation in all community systems, especially the media
- gender inequalities in the management of natural resources and the safeguarding of the environment
- persistent discrimination against and violation of the rights of female children

The Conference's mission statement includes these sentences: "Equality between women and men is a matter of human rights and a condition for social justice and is also a necessary and fundamental prerequisite for equality, development and peace . . . equality between women and men is a condition . . . for society to meet the challenges of the twenty-first century." This series provides examples of how women have risen above adversity, despite their disadvantaged social, economic, and political positions.

Each book in WOMEN'S ISSUES: GLOBAL TRENDS takes a look at women's lives in a different key region or culture, revealing the history, contributions, triumphs, and challenges of women around the world. Women play key roles in shaping families, spirituality, and societies. By interweaving historic backdrops with the modern-day evolving role of women in the home and in society at large, this series presents the important part women play as cultural

communicators. Protection of women's rights is an integral part of universal human rights, peace, and economic security. As a result, readers who gain understanding of women's lives around the world will have deeper insight into the current condition of global interactions.

AUTHOR'S PREFACE

As I write this book, I try to imagine how you, the reader, might receive it. I write a passage and think, "How will this sound to a boy? To a girl? To a person from the religion I am describing? To a person in another religion? To an atheist?" A book about religion and gender touches on life's most important issues—self-identity, morals, the choices that determine what we will make of our lives.

If you truly believe in some spiritual faith, you are bound to have strong feelings about it. You will be upset if you feel I wrote something critical of your religion. If you experience your faith as different from the way I make it sound, that will also concern you. It may be you have strong negative reactions toward a religion discussed in this book—either because it was a negative part of your own past, or because you perceive it as a threat to the values you treasure. You may think I am promoting, or being too positive about someone else's religion. No one writes in a vacuum, and I do have my own personal faith, which is very important to me. If I were a person of no religious faith, that would also impact my understanding. I can assure you, however, that I have tried my level best to be even-handed in every chapter of this book.

Even within the same religion, women can see things very differently indeed. One woman's perfect existence may be another's worst nightmare. For this reason, in each chapter I have presented a variety of women's viewpoints within the particular spiritual tradition.

You might be disappointed that your religion only received a brief notice—or it does not appear in this book at all. There are many more religious groups

Spiritual faith gives a deeper meaning to many women's lives.

that certainly deserve to be discussed, but because of the book's length, only ten major groups could be represented.

Whatever your perspective on religion and gender, this book's goal is to give you a deeper understanding of the spiritual faiths that give meaning to the lives of women around you. As you gain a wider understanding of others' viewpoints, you will find that your own thinking is enriched. Best of all, understanding builds bridges of respect and tolerance.

"YOU MADE ADAM AND YOU GAVE HIM HIS WIFE EVE TO BE HIS
HELP AND SUPPORT;
AND FROM THESE TWO THE HUMAN RACE DESCENDED. YOU SAID,
'IT IS NOT GOOD FOR THE MAN TO BE ALONE; LET US MAKE HIM A
PARTNER LIKE HIMSELF.'"
—TOBIT 8:6-7, NEW AMERICAN BIBLE

1

In many ways Rachael Lampa is like any other seventeen-year-old girl. She's excited about getting her driver's license and going through her senior year; her favorite actor is Adam Sandler; she enjoys listening to Dave Matthews Band; and she plays on the girls' basketball team.

Rachael is not entirely ordinary, though: she is a popular singer with enormous success in the Christian music market. She has performed before thousands and appeared live on Jay Leno. Yet when asked what she is most thankful for, Rachael doesn't think of the success or the fame. She says she is grateful for: "An awesome, supportive family and friends . . . the privilege to have grown up with faith and the knowledge of God."

A highlight in her life was the opportunity she had on August 7, 2000, when Rachael performed for the Pope and a crowd of more than two million Catholic young people gathered for World Youth Day from over 150 nations. On a more everyday level as well, the Catholic Church plays a vital role in Rachael Lampa's Christian faith.

Catholics are the largest single group of Christians in North America. In Canada, they are 12.8 million people, or 43 percent of the population. There are approximately 51 million Catholics in the United States as of 2003. Of these, more than 27 million are women.

To understand the Catholic Church and its influence in women's lives, we have to first look at Christianity in general. Christianity began with the life of one man, Jesus of Nazareth, recorded in four books known as the Gospels. The Gospels tell of Jesus' *miraculous* birth, his teachings, and miracles. Special detail is given to Jesus' death on the cross. Most Christians believe that Jesus' death made peace between God and humanity. After the crucifixion, Jesus appeared to his followers, resurrected. At the conclusion of Matthew's Gospel, Jesus promises, "I am with you always, even to the end of time."

Jesus had very high regard for women. Marcus Borg, one of today's leading Jesus scholars, says:

> One of the most remarkable features of Jesus' ministry was his relationship to women. Challenging the *conventional* wisdom of his time, it continues to challenge the conventional wisdom of much of the church.

For almost a thousand years after Jesus' death, the Christian church was a single worldwide religion. Various groups have parted ways since then, but today's Catholic Church traces its major beliefs and practices back to this original *universal* church. (The word "catholic" means universal). Bishops, all of whom are male, provide authority. Foremost among them is the Pope, who also serves as spokesman for the entire church.

Women in North America today vary greatly in their views of the church. Some Catholic ideas, such as prohibiting birth control and allowing only male priests, have been criticized as *sexist*. At the same time, however, the Catholic

Church holds a very high view of the Virgin Mary, exalting a woman for her role in humanity's salvation.

The Catechism of the Catholic Church states, "The Virgin Mary is acknowledged and honored as being truly the Mother of God and of the redeemer. She is clearly the mother of the members of Christ." Many Catholics believe Mary continues to play a vital role in the world.

Beverly Donofrio, best known for her book *Riding in Cars with Boys,* also wrote *Looking for Mary* where she talks about her difficulties relating to God. She goes on to say, "I responded most strongly to a woman. A mother was what I desired—softness, gentle care, compassion. . . . And so Mary remained my focus."

Although the number of nuns has recently declined, the Catholic Church has a special role for women devoted to the religious life. In 1965, more than 180,000 nuns served in the United States; now, they are less than 84,000. Changes in society have greatly reduced the popularity of *religious orders.* Many women find a career more appealing than religious life. In a society that glamorizes sexual relationships, the choice of lifelong *celibacy* is unappealing.

Meanwhile, the religious orders have changed, along with the rest of North America. Most nuns today don't wear habits. Many live in normal apartments or houses. Despite these changes, nuns continue to serve church and society in some powerful ways.

Lucy Kaylin's book *For the Love of God* tells true stories of today's nuns. For instance, few people know there is actually a religious order called the Little Sisters of Jesus, who serve Christ in a circus! Carson & Barnes circus is a big show—five rings, huge tent, lots of wild animals, and many people who work for the circus, sometimes doing dangerous stunts. The Little Sisters of Jesus work alongside others at the circus, repairing things, taking up and putting away the show, and manning the concession stands. Amid the noise and crazi-

Catholics emphasize Mary's spritual role.

ness of the carnival life, their goal is "to establish a prayerful presence in the circus."

The Dwelling Place is another ministry run by sisters described in *For the Love of God*. In one of the worst parts of New York City, these nuns serve meals for up to two hundred women at a time. The sisters have been punched and even bitten by desperate people whom they are trying to help. Yet they continue to serve with compassion. The nuns counsel drug addicts and homeless women, hug and feed them, and find jobs and homes for them.

Of course, being a nun isn't just about helping people. Those who have chosen to become religious sisters find their lives are more focused, more meaningful, and more spiritual than they would have been otherwise. One sister says, "I think of God as the ocean. You can look at how beautiful it is from the beach, or you can go swimming in it. I had the desire to just be a fish."

While many women feel truly blessed by their Catholic faith, some aspects of Catholicism have caused questioning or disagreement from the church's female members. Most dramatic are issues of birth control. The Catholic Church is clearly opposed to legalized abortion. "Human life must be respected and protected absolutely from the moment of *conception*," says the *Catechism of the Catholic Church*.

Abortion is a *controversial* topic among North Americans in general, and American and Canadian Catholics often disagree with the official teachings of the church. Surveys taken in 1998 and 2002 show a majority of U.S. Catholics favor legalized abortion. In Canada, despite the huge numbers of Catholics in the population, there is no political party opposed to abortion. These trends show that even devout Catholics in North America disagree in large numbers with official church teaching.

The Catholic Church offers a special form of holy orders for women who wish to commit their lives to God.

If abortion causes disagreement between some Catholic women and the church, the issue of birth control causes almost universal disagreement with church teaching. In 1968, the church released a document titled, *Humanae Vitae*, which made it clear that artificial methods of birth control (such as the pill, diaphragm, or condom) are unacceptable for Catholics. Pope John Paul II has said contraceptive practices are "*intrinsically evil.*" Despite such strong condemnation from the church, 96 percent of Catholic couples in the United States in a recent survey admitted their use of contraceptives.

Thomas Fox, in his book *Sexuality and Catholicism*, notes one reason for the difference between official church teaching and the opinions of North American Catholics: "It is women who are dominated by men, women who become pregnant, women who carry the unborn, and women who give birth." Nonetheless, it is only "men's voices" that make authoritative decisions for the Catholic Church.

The issue of women's **ordination** is another point where many Catholic women in the United States and Canada find themselves at odds with their church. For centuries, only men have been allowed to serve as priests. A recent survey found that two out of three Canadian Catholics say their church's view of sex roles in the church is "outdated." A 2002 survey in the United States found similar results.

In 1979, Sister Theresa Kane had the opportunity to speak before 5,000 nuns who had gathered in a Washington, D.C., shrine to greet the new Pope, John Paul II. In a loud, clear voice she begged the Pope, in front of her sisters, to "be mindful of the intense suffering that is part of the life of many women in these United States." She went on to say that respect for women's dignity should include the rights of women to serve "in all ministries of the church." There was no response from the Pope at that time. In 1993, the Pope issued a document titled *On Priestly Ordination*. That document contains the strongest

Although nuns were traditionally pictured as demure, quiet women, many historical "sisters" were strong voices who spoke out for change in their societies. Today's nuns also provide leadership for their church.

statement of the church opposing female priests. The Pope says that the issue is "definitively" settled.

Despite the church's official position on females, common practice in the United States allows girls, along with boys, to assist priests serving Mass. This has been well received in most congregations. As one woman worshiping in a Wisconsin church put it: "This [altar service] opens windows for our children. There are times when, as women, we feel we're not always appreciated in the *hierarchy* of the church, but it's generally the women who pass the faith along." Late in 2003, however, reports were publicized that the Vatican might prohibit the use of altar girls.

Though barred from the priesthood, a surprising number of women have found ways to provide practical leadership in Catholic congregations. North America lacks enough priests to serve all the churches. To compensate for this shortage, congregations hire "pastoral administrators"—men and women who serve under the local priest to oversee the finances and committees of a congregation, and to provide counseling, hospital visitation, or practical assistance to congregational members. In some congregations, these people deliver the homily (a short message explaining the daily Bible passage) and say prayers during services. The one thing a pastoral administrator cannot do is lead *sacramental* rituals. In the United States, approximately 16,000 women serve in Catholic churches as pastoral administrators.

In one Houston church, Charles Morris, author of the book *American Catholic*, asked a woman what she thought about women priests. She replied, "We already run the church."

The role of pastoral administrators is likely to expand, because the shortage of priests is not lessening. What's more, at the start of the twenty-first century, Catholic Churches in the United States and Canada faced a mounting tide of lawsuits and angry accusations. Hundreds of priests have been accused of child

Many of the Catholic Church's saints are women.

WOMEN IN NORTH AMERICA'S RELIGIOUS WORLD

molestation and sexual *victimization* of the people they serve. The scandal has made many young men even more reluctant to enter the priesthood.

Although the beliefs, practices, and abuses of their church trouble some Catholic women, dissatisfaction is only part of the picture. For every woman who feels restricted by the church's teachings, there is another who finds great satisfaction in traditional beliefs. Female speakers and authors have argued that the Pope's views of women's roles, birth control, and *sanctity* of life are positive teachings for women. Does restricting sexual expression protect women or limit them? Are laws protecting unborn children necessarily *antifeminist?* Devout Catholic women are divided in their answers to these questions. Even women who disagree strongly with the church on a particular issue will also express their loyalty to the Catholic faith as a whole. Most North American Catholics believe they can disagree at some points, while still supporting the church.

In November of 2003, 23,000 teenagers worshipped with more than forty bishops and a hundred priests at a Catholic Youth Conference in a Houston stadium. Rachael Lampa was at the conference to lead her peers in song. As the event drew to a close, she was enthusiastic. "It's great to see thousands of kids on fire for God!" she exclaimed. Catholic women in North America may have many questions regarding the future of their church. Yet the enthusiasm of Rachael and her peers shows the continuing faith and vitality of Catholic women in North America.

"YOU ARE ALL CHILDREN OF GOD THROUGH FAITH IN JESUS CHRIST...
THERE IS NEITHER JEW NOR GREEK, SLAVE NOR FREE, MALE NOR FEMALE,
FOR YOU ARE ALL ONE IN JESUS CHRIST."
—GALATIANS 3:28, NEW INTERNATIONAL VERSION: INCLUSIVE
LANGUAGE EDITION OF THE BIBLE

2

WOMEN IN NORTH AMERICA'S EVANGELICAL CHURCHES

Anne Graham Lotz is a gifted communicator who calls her audience to a personal relationship with God. She is also the daughter of world famous evangelist Billy Graham and his wife Ruth Bell Graham. Anne learned as a young woman that she had a talent for teaching the Bible to others. As a result, she received many invitations to speak at Christian gatherings.

Even with extraordinary talent and an extraordinary family heritage, Anne has struggled with the challenges faced by Evangelical women. One time she was asked to speak at a conference for pastors. Many of those in attendance were opposed to women preaching. During that conference dozens of pastors stood up and turned their backs to her. She recalled a Bible verse, Jeremiah 1:17—"Therefore prepare yourself and arise, and speak to them all that I command you. Do not be dismayed before their faces"—and she applied that verse to herself. "Only God was telling me not to be afraid of their backs."

She has addressed thousands of pastors and missionaries, and she is the focal point of an international ministry. When America needed solace after the

Evangelical women emphasize their individual relationship with God.

terrorist attacks of September 11, 2001, television news stations turned to Anne for interviews. Yet she has never served as pastor in a church, because she comes from a tradition that denies women the authority to preach. In many ways, Anne Graham Lotz represents both the opportunities and the limitations of women in North America's Evangelical churches at the start of the twenty-first century.

Evangelical Christians emphasize the need for a personal relationship with God; they define the foundation of this relationship as "accepting Jesus Christ as Savior." According to Evangelical thinking, when a person asks Christ into her heart, she becomes "born again" and embarks on a changed life.

Evangelicals also regard the Bible as the divinely *inspired* Word of God, believed to be free of mistakes in whatever it teaches. Many Evangelicals spend a daily "quiet time" reading the Bible and expecting God to communicate with them through its pages. Informal prayer—talking to God about everyday needs—is also an important part of Evangelical spirituality.

For Evangelicals, the heart of their faith is a life-changing personal encounter with Christ. People who have had such experiences are often eager to share their stories. For example, a woman named Vicki relates her salvation experience. She says, "As a result of the sexual abuse and violence that occurred [in my life], it led me into a path of destructive behavior and a life of utter confusion and feelings of inadequacy." She drank and took drugs, cut herself, had an abortion, and drifted in and out of psychiatric hospitals. In March of 1995, a friend invited Vicki to church, and Vicki became so convinced God was real that she called on Him to help her. She now says, "I have completely healed, recovered and overcome in every area! Whatever a person has gone through or may be facing right now, they can get through it just like I did. God will heal you, strengthen you and take care of your every need."

Evangelicals believe that the Bible is literally and completely true.

The exact number of Evangelicals in North America is difficult to count, because Evangelicalism is a matter of individual belief, rather than membership in a certain kind of church. Estimates of Evangelicals' numbers vary greatly, but there may be 24 million Evangelical Christians in the United States alone.

Though this form of Christianity began with the Puritans, American Evangelicalism was later influenced greatly by religious "revivals" that swept through America in the 1700s and 1800s. As the twentieth century began, events took place that would overshadow all previous religious revivals.

In 1901, a handful of Bible students in Topeka, Kansas, experienced a phenomenon they called "speaking in tongues." This event recalled the Bible's description of *Pentecost*, recorded in Acts chapter 2. As a result, those who spoke in tongues became known as "Pentecostals." The "Pentecostal" revival of the early twentieth century caught its second wind in the 1960s with the

"Charismatic" movement. Worldwide, more than 400 million Christians now claim to be either "Pentecostal" or "Charismatic."

Pentecostal church services typically include lively modern music and joyful, exuberant expressions of faith. In their daily lives, Pentecostal and Charismatic Christians expect to experience God's supernatural power.

Evangelicals today place no restrictions on women's roles in business, education, or politics. Christian career women are encouraged to pursue excellence as a way to glorify God. Until recently, however, most Evangelicals have opposed women's leadership in their churches. They based this position on 1 Timothy 2:12, in the New Testament, where the Apostle Paul says he does not allow women to "teach or have authority over men" in church. A few Evangelicals have made exceptions to this rule, however. Some have pointed to passages such as Galatians 3:28, where the same Apostle says there is no distinction between men and women, "for you are all one in Christ."

Women have made significant contributions to North American Evangelical history. In 1880, the Salvation Army sent their first team of *evangelists* from Great Britain to America. All seven missionaries were women, who became known as "the Hallelujah Gals." They preached in the streets, near saloons, and in the roughest parts of squalid cities. Often, they were greeted with jeers, threats, thrown food, and sometimes violence. Despite such opposition, they established ten churches in three months, conducting more than two hundred services each week. Their success prompted Salvation Army cofounder William Booth to exclaim, "My best men are women."

Another important woman in Evangelical history is Aimee Semple McPherson, born in a farmhouse in Ontario, Canada, in 1890. Her mother, a member of the Salvation Army, had asked God to give her a daughter who would become a mighty evangelist. Aimee became skeptical of the Bible as a teen, but in 1908 she was converted and spoke in *tongues*. She married a mis-

sionary and traveled with him to China. Her husband died there of illness, and she returned to America a broken young woman. Soon after that, however, she received her own "call" to preach.

"Sister Aimee" was an enormous hit. Accompanied by her mother and little daughter, she was the first woman to drive a car from coast to coast across the United States. Huge crowds came to her tent meetings to become born again or receive miraculous healing. Settling in Los Angeles in the 1920s, she ordered construction of Angelus Temple—one of the largest churches in America at that time. She started a Christian radio station, and was the first woman to be broadcast on a weekly radio show. In many ways, the large Evangelical churches that are popular throughout America today have followed the pattern set by Aimee McPherson. In her time, she was America's best known Christian speaker. When she died, she had established 410 churches with 29,000 members.

Evangelicals today are still divided on women's roles in churches and in families. Some believe men should have authority over women, both in homes and in churches. On the other hand, other Evangelicals insist that either women or men can exercise leadership.

How should husbands and wives settle differences in their homes? Many Evangelicals say wives should submit to their husbands, and some women insist they are happy with this arrangement. As one wife says, "My freedom comes from letting my husband be in charge." But not all Evangelicals agree. Bible scholar Gordon Fee does not believe that a marriage has to have one partner in authority over the other. For forty-five years, he asserts, he and his wife have happily arrived at mutual agreements.

Today's Evangelicals also hold differing views of women's leadership in churches. The Southern Baptist Convention officially stated in 2000 that,

"While both men and women are gifted for service in the church, the office of pastor is limited to men as qualified by Scripture." On the other hand, America's largest church, Willow Creek, encourages women to serve along with men as pastors.

Evangelical women who serve as foreign missionaries perform all the duties of their male counterparts—both in charitable work and teaching the Bible. Perhaps due to the scarcity of these workers, the limitations that churches in North America impose on women don't seem to apply to missionaries. Women's messages are sometimes called "missionary sharing" rather than preaching—but they contain the same content a sermon would.

World-famous Evangelical Billy Graham was once asked, "If a woman feels the call to mission, is gifted for ministry and leadership and comes up against a solid wall of resistance, what advice would you give her?" He replied, "If God is leading her, she shouldn't take no for an answer."

While Evangelical churches continue to debate women's roles, many Evangelical women sidestep such issues, focusing attention instead on how they can best serve God. Jill Briscoe serves as minister at Elmbrook Church in Milwaukee. Like many of her sisters in the faith, she is aware of her talents and determined to use them for Christ. At the same time, she tries to avoid conflict—advising other born-again women to use their gifts in whatever ways their own church allows. She says, "Personally, I believe I first have to answer to God for his gifts and calling on my life. I don't want to get to heaven and hear him say, 'Half-done, thou half-faithful servant.'"

"HUSBANDS, LOVE YOUR WIVES, EVEN AS CHRIST ALSO LOVED THE CHURCH,
AND GAVE HIMSELF FOR IT."
—EPHESIANS 5:25, KING JAMES VERSION OF THE BIBLE

WOMEN IN THE MORMON CHURCH

When Mary Ellen Smoot and her husband were called to a meeting with Gordon B. Hinckley, the president of the Mormon Church, Mary Ellen had no idea she would become president of a women's organization claiming more than four million members. Hinckley told her he believed she was called to lead the worldwide Church Relief Society. She was amazed, but willingly accepted the job.

"When a prophet of the Lord lays his hands on your head, you feel like you can do anything," she said. Smoot, quoted in the Ogden, Utah, *Standard Examiner*, says she wants Mormon women to set an example by their countenance: "I don't see women in the world as happy women, we need to learn to be happy women."

Millions of Mormon women are apparently happy with their faith. The Church of Jesus Christ of Latter Day Saints (LDS), known informally as the

Mormons, is one of the fastest growing religions in America—and in the world. In the United States, there are almost 5 million LDS members; numbers in Canada are much lower, with only 151,000 members, but there are more than 11 million Mormons worldwide. Globally, the church is growing faster than a million members every three years. This is due to the efforts of more than 60,000 young missionaries, working in more than a hundred countries.

Despite its enormous success, the Mormon Church has generated controversy on a number of issues—including the role of women. A former president of the Church Relief Society explained the LDS view of a woman's ideal role: "A woman should give her greatest priority to her home: her husband, her family, and the opportunity for child-bearing. That is her divine mission." Many women claim to find great satisfaction in the clearly defined boundaries set for them in the Mormon faith.

Yet not all are happy. One young woman, who eventually left the LDS Church, describes her experience: "I saw these women expending their mental and physical energy. . . . Each trying to be the perfect wife, mother, daughter. . . . I saw the married women struggling with endless childbirths, denying their professional desires and talents." In October of 2000, more than fifty Mormon women signed an open letter to the LDS Church and published it in the *Salt Lake Tribune*. They said:

> Many Mormon women have expressed profound dissatisfaction for generations, privately and publicly, loudly and clearly, in print and in person, alone and in numbers. Thus, we write to correct a misconception repeatedly set forth by LDS Church leaders in the Media: Mormon women are not content; we do have complaints.

The Church of Jesus Christ of Latter Day Saints is a uniquely American religion that began in rural New York State. Joseph Smith, the founder, was born

in 1805. In 1823, he reported a vision, in which he saw an angel. Smith said, "He called me by name, and said unto me that he was a messenger sent from God; and that his name was Moroni; that God had work for me to do." The angel went on to explain: "There was a book deposited, written upon gold plates, giving an account of the former inhabitants of this continent . . . the fullness of the everlasting Gospel was contained in it."

The Book of Mormon, given to Joseph Smith by the angel Moroni, tells how Jews came to North America in the centuries before Christ and became the ancestors of today's American Indians. Smith later came forth with more writings called *Doctrine and Covenants* and *The Pearl of Great Price*. These books, together with the King James Translation of the Holy Bible, are the sacred scriptures of the Latter Day Saints Church.

Despite numerous conflicts with "gentiles" (non-Mormons), Joseph Smith gained many followers. He and his group moved to Missouri and then Illinois, where Smith was *martyred* and Brigham Young assumed leadership of the group. Young led a covered wagon migration to Utah, where the greatest concentrations of Mormons live to this day.

Smith and several other important leaders had multiple wives, some of whom were just teenagers. When the church resettled in the Utah frontier, *polygamy* became common among the Mormons. Brigham Young, for example, had more than fifty wives.

The U.S. government was opposed to the practice, and hundreds of Mormons were jailed. Mormon leaders could see that polygamy would result in the end of the church. In 1890, a new addition was made to *The Doctrine and Covenants*, and polygamy was forbidden. Since then, the LDS church has quickly removed from membership any members claiming more than one wife.

Latter Day Saints believe the full truth about God was hidden from the world until the angel revealed it to Joseph Smith. They also believe God was

once human like we are, but he grew in knowledge and power to become a divine being. LDS president Lorenzo Snow explains: "As man is, God once was; as God is, man may become." According to Mormon teaching, God's plan is to exalt mortals after death, so that "they shall be gods, because they have all power" (*Doctrine and Covenants*, 132).

Mormon's believe heaven has three levels, each more desirable than the last. To be "exalted" to the highest realm, men and women not only have to live holy lives, but they also have to be married in an LDS temple. Marriage is thus very important. In the heavenly life, states Mormon teaching, couples who have achieved divine status will rule over new worlds and populate them with children of their own.

Another important concept related to male and female roles is the priesthood. LDS churches don't have paid ministers or priests. Instead, any adult male member of the church who is willing to follow the required behaviors can become a member of the "priesthood." The vast majority of Mormon men do so.

A priest's most important role is that of husband and father. In the temple marriage ceremony, the groom reaches through a partition and draws his wife to him, symbolizing his role of summoning her to share eternal life with him. He confers blessings on his children and his wife in this life, and he will govern all of his descendants in the life to come. Birth control is discouraged, since couples should bear many children to reign with them in heaven.

Though only males serve as priests, women are advised to "get the best education they can in order to earn their own living." Utah, with its large Mormon population, was the second state to grant women the right to vote, and Martha Hughes Cannon, a Mormon, was the first woman in the United States elected to serve as a state senator. Another Mormon, Jean Westwood, was the first woman to serve as chairperson for the National Democratic Party. In Mormon

churches, women preside over the significant benevolent work of the Relief Societies.

The Latter Day Saints Church is famous for its "missionaries"—young people who go from door to door recruiting for their church. Young men can do missionary work at age nineteen and serve for two full years, while women have to wait until age twenty-one and serve only eighteen months. Only one out of five Mormon missionaries is a woman, since the majority of LDS women are already married by age twenty-one, and missionaries have to be single. Trisha Randall, a twenty-three-year-old former Mormon missionary to the Czech Republic, explains, "The church would say you should not put off marriage just to go on a mission; you should only go if it really feels right."

Some Mormon women feel dissatisfied with their religion—but at the same time, they may derive a sense of spiritual satisfaction from their private religious practices.

While women have some latitude in their roles, the Mormon Church places greatest emphasis on the woman's role in a family. As an official LDS Web site explains: "Mormon women have the specific responsibility to be righteous daughters of God; good, faithful wives; and loving mothers." Deborah Laake says in her book *Secret Ceremonies*: "Marriage is the background of Mormon society and doctrine." Students at Mormon colleges are routinely encouraged by faculty members to look for mates. Many female members of the LDS Church claim to find fulfillment in this traditional role.

Covenant Communications, a Mormon publishing company, sells books for a growing market—Mormon romance novels. Unlike common romance novels, "Sex is not an appeal at all," says Robby Nichols, vice president of marketing for the publishing firm. "Commitment is what's strong in our market. There is no swearing, no graphic anything, and we steer as far from innuendo as we can."

Deborah Laake was one of those romantic young Mormons in her years at Brigham Young University. But, as she chronicles in *Secret Ceremonies*, her dreams turned sour. She married in college because her boyfriend said he had received a message from God that they should do so. She didn't love him, however, and she was then increasingly depressed in a marriage where her husband treated her as every way inferior. After divorcing, she was barred from attending the temple and humiliated by having to divulge details of her private life to Church authorities. She finally left the church, tired of "priesthood leaders . . . who *sanctioned* me for nothing, who were smug or patronizing or bullying or unhearing."

While many LDS women are glowing in their endorsement of their church and families, there are others who, like Deborah Laake, struggle with the faith. Kent Ponder, Ph.D., is a psychologist, who has done research with hundreds of LDS Church members. He notes:

Utah residents currently use more antidepressants than the residents of any other U.S. state. This problem is clearly, closely and definitely linked to the Church of Jesus Christ of Latter-day Saints. . . . The same LDS Church that works so well for many works very badly for many others, who become chronically depressed, *especially women*. Studies indicate that women suffer twice as much depression as men. These individuals then cope with their chronic mental pain and depression by using antidepressant drugs and/or treatment by LDS therapists, who too often treat them ignorantly and counterproductively.

One of Dr. Ponder's daughters, who was raised and married in the LDS Church, explains: "It's so counter-intuitive for women, so full of gender unfairness and contradictions. And to have any real difference of opinion means having to go against every person in your [church] community."

Despite opposition, some LDS women have spoken out for greater equality in the church. Maxine Hanks was excommunicated (forced to leave) from the church for publishing her belief that Joseph Smith intended women, as well as men, to serve in the priesthood. She writes:

Although women's authority is plainly evident in Mormon history, today's male church leaders won't acknowledge it, for that would mean having to take responsibility for the sins of their fathers and grandfathers . . . instead, they blame Christ.

She sees the LDS Church as an institution where "hostility to women manifests in subtle and shocking ways." She concludes a letter to the *Los Angeles Times* by saying: "Whether today's women can reclaim their authority and priesthood in the church and fully participate remains a question; first, they must find authority within themselves. But I will not 'come back' to a church that crushes female authority and individual conscience."

Some women who were raised Mormon have left the church. They may feel a sense of isolation and bitterness—or they may be able to reclaim a spiritual reality on their own.

Mary Ellen Smoot, the president of the Church Relief Society, however, wastes little time worrying about Mormon gender issues. She says, "I don't think our women want the priesthood." And then she adds that even if women wished to, "You cannot change the Savior's Church."

"HER WAYS ARE WAYS OF PLEASANTNESS, AND ALL HER PATHS ARE PEACE."
— PROVERBS 3:17, NEW REVISED STANDARD VERSION OF THE BIBLE

4

AMISH AND MENNONITE WOMEN

Louise Stoltzfus recalls an experience she had at six years of age when her mother tied the family's horse and buggy to a fence and asked Louise and her four young brothers to wait in the buggy while she ran back inside to get another child. As they waited, a car stopped and a man jumped out with a camera. He asked if the children would stand by the buggy and pose, and then he took their pictures, smiled, and gave them each a dime before leaving. In her book *Amish Women*, Louise writes: "Yes, our privacy had been invaded. Yes, we were delighted with the dimes. Yes, such experiences are typical."

Amish women and men dress distinctively, and in many ways live differently, from the larger society around them. Visitors to Amish country immediately notice the women with their hair covered by bonnets, the men in straw hats and suspenders, and families clopping down the road in black horse-drawn buggies. The faith of the Amish calls them to live "in the world but not of the world."

Ironically, their desire to be free from the outside world has attracted enormous attention and misunderstanding. More than any religious group in America, the Amish are *stereotyped* and mocked. Amish women are too often seen as nameless curiosities in old-fashioned garb, rather than individuals with their own unique lives, struggles, and contributions to the world.

The Old Order Amish are only one part of a larger spiritual family, the Anabaptists. Anabaptists include Amish, Mennonite, Brethren, and Bruderhoff denominations. Mennonite and Brethren women in America today may be of African American, Central American, and Indonesian descent—among others. One works as a lawyer in Los Angeles, another as a professor in a Midwestern college, and another as pastor in a growing urban church on the East Coast. Women who follow various forms of Anabaptist faith are as varied as the many-colored mosaic of North American life in the twenty-first century. Yet they all follow a time-honored tradition of peacefully following the teachings of Jesus Christ.

The Amish lifestyle is very different from the
culture familiar to most twenty-first-century North Americans.

Making an accurate count of the Amish is not easy, but estimates suggest more than 144,000 members in North America. They live in twenty-two American states, and in Ontario province in Canada. Meanwhile, more than 520,000 Mennonites live in North America, and of these, 230,000 live in Canada. Mennonite congregations exist in every state and province of the United States and Canada.

The Anabaptist faith began in the sixteenth century. At that time, Martin Luther led a number of churches away from Catholicism, giving birth to today's Protestant churches. The Anabaptists, however, differed from both Protestants and Catholics. While other Christians of the time believed government rulers should make laws concerning religious worship, the Anabaptists thought there should be separation between church and state. They were the first Christians to set forth this principle, which is one of the founding truths of the United States.

Anabaptists also believe Christians must practice nonviolence. They take Jesus' command·to "love your enemies" very literally. Amish, Mennonite, and Brethren Christians refuse to take up arms and kill as policemen or soldiers. Many serve in organizations dedicated to world peace.

Anabaptists also differed from Protestants and Catholics regarding baptism. Where other sixteenth-century churches baptized newborn babies, the Anabaptists believed individuals should choose whether to join a church and be baptized, after reaching an age when an independent personal decision was possible. People who had been baptized as babies decided to be baptized again when they joined Anabaptist churches. This was known as "re-baptizing" and hence the term "Ana" (or "re") baptists.

For more than a hundred years, Catholics and Protestants killed each other in religious wars. They also tortured and slaughtered thousands of Anabaptists.

Some were burned alive, others had their flesh peeled off and their tongues cut out. But the Anabaptists would not respond with violence.

When the movement was faltering, a Dutch minister named Menno Simons organized and inspired the survivors. The Mennonite church is named after him. The Amish began as a group that split-off from the Mennonites; their founder was Jacob Amman.

Around 1700, many Amish and Mennonites came to America. They originally settled in Pennsylvania, where they found an unusual degree of religious tolerance.

Today, the Old Order Amish groups are the most conservative Anabaptist churches. Members do not own or use automobiles or electric appliances. They

have reasons for their choices: cars cause families to move away from each other, and they also cause many deaths. Televisions reduce the time people spend talking and doing things together. The Amish shape their society by making radical choices against elements of North American culture that can be destructive.

In the past, almost all Amish women and men lived and worked on their own family's farmland. Today, many Amish work outside their farms. In northern Indiana in 1970, two-thirds of the Amish men were involved in farming; today, only a third are farmers. Most work in Indiana's mobile-home manufacturing industry.

This has caused difficulties for Amish mothers. The Amish do not practice birth control, and many Amish women have eight to ten children. In past generations, fathers would supervise some of the children during the day, and this allowed mothers to care for their babies. Now, however, women are caring for their large families by themselves, while the men go out to work. Women must also do gardening and housework. As one Amish mother says, "I need him [my husband] so there is at least one parent who isn't too tired and stressed out to answer [the children's] questions decently." These Amish women struggle with the challenge of rearing many young children and doing all the housework by themselves, while at the same time they have no way to prevent large families. In the past, childbirth meant that Amish women had to confront the unfamiliarity and sterile coldness of North American hospitals. In the 1950s, however, a doctor named Grace Kaiser began practicing among the Amish in Pennsylvania's Lancaster County. Known affectionately as "Dochtah Frau" (Doctor Woman), she delivered many babies in Amish homes. Now there are professional midwives who serve the Amish community. As one Amish mother, Naomi, puts it in the book *Amish Women*, "I love having my children at home. It is so convenient. So natural. So normal."

Outsiders tend to look at Amish people and assume their lives are both terribly old-fashioned and unhappy, or else assume they live in an ideal state of peaceful, unworldly happiness. Both stereotypes fail to grasp Amish reality. As one Amish woman admits, "We Amish are not perfect. All the elements of life which are morally wrong are present in our society. We are not free of any human problem." At the same time, many Amish women find their lifestyle satisfying. They have to work harder, lacking modern conveniences—but this improves their health. According to research, Amish women have stronger hearts, lower weight, and overall better health than the general population. Studies also show they are more satisfied with their appearance than other American women. They eat well, exercise constantly, and don't feel pressured to compare themselves to skinny fashion models.

More than 95 percent of Amish women choose to join the church when given that choice at adulthood. All children—of both sexes—are free to leave the Amish community if they wish, before they choose to become baptized and join the church at the age of twenty-one. Most join the church because they desire the benefits of membership.

Amish women are not as isolated as non-Amish people imagine them to be. They can shop at Wal-Mart, ride Greyhound buses, visit doctors, dentists, and other professionals. They cannot fly to Europe, because airplanes are frowned upon. Yet they can take a cruise on an ocean liner. They have no phones in their homes, but public phones are mounted on poles near farms, in order to make emergency calls or arrange for a taxi. Amish women cannot own cars, yet they are free to take the buggy or call a taxi whenever they wish. In addition, they experience something important that is missing from many lives in the twenty-first century—a sense of community.

Amish women belong to a strong, closely knit supportive community. They don't have Social Security benefits, life insurance, or health insurance—but all

their needs from cradle to grave will be fully taken care of by their church. Most Amish women do not consider themselves "trapped" in an old-fashioned lifestyle. They are living in a way that makes sense to them, a way that fits their Christian faith, a way they have chosen. Living in close-knit church communities gives Amish women strong support for their faith.

A speeding driver killed an Amish teenager as the boy was crossing the road in front of his family farm. As police and other professionals gathered at the scene, the driver of the car was crying and shaking. The boy's mother and father tried to comfort the driver: "We do not blame you for what has happened today." This amazing ability to forgive is the fruit of the centuries-old Anabaptist faith.

Other Anabaptist women live in ways that differ from the Amish. Hutterite (also known as Bruderhoff) Christians live in carefully planned *communes*. They work and eat together, but they use computers and other high-tech conveniences. The Beachy Amish Church allows members to own cars and electric appliances—yet still follows customs unique to the Amish. Most Mennonite and Brethren women live the same as other American women.

The prayer veil is the most common form of distinctive attire still worn by some Mennonite women. This is a small round piece of white cloth, worn on the back of the head. Yolanda Martin, a Mennonite college student, writes in an online article, "I get many stares and second glances various places I go. I look different than the rest of society because of my head covering." She goes on to explain:

> Mennonites believe that a woman's head should be covered when she prays, according to 1 Corinthians 11. . . . Since we are commanded to pray continually (1 Thessalonians 5:17) or pray whenever the need arises, women generally keep their heads covered all the time.

The Mennonite Confession of Faith, in its footnotes, affirms the full equality of men and women. "God created both man and woman in the divine image. The rule of man over woman is a result of sin and is therefore not an acceptable order among the redeemed." In 1911, Ann Allebach became the first Mennonite woman to be ordained as a pastor. Since then, many other women have accepted the pastoral call in Mennonite Churches.

Mennonite and Brethren Christians are known for the amazing amount of work that they do providing food, education, disaster relief, and other forms of aid to people around the world. When hurricanes ravage Honduras and Florida, when starvation hits Bangladesh and Ethiopia, and when wars cause destruction in Afghanistan and Columbia, Mennonites help rebuild, bringing order and comfort out of chaos.

In Kamloops, British Columbia, twenty-three teenagers volunteered to help Mennonite Disaster Service (MDS) rebuild a home for a family stricken by fire. Three of the girls sifted through ash on their hands and knees searching for something precious that belonged to the owner of the burned home—her wedding ring. Incredibly, they found it. The three girls were "on cloud nine" according to their MDS supervisor. They were glad to know that "God used them in a compassionate way."

"THAT LITTLE MAN IN BLACK THERE SAY A WOMAN CAN'T HAVE AS
MUCH RIGHTS AS A MAN CAUSE CHRIST WASN'T A WOMAN. WHERE DID
YOUR CHRIST COME FROM? FROM GOD AND WOMAN! MAN HAD
NOTHING TO DO WITH HIM!"
—SOJOURNER TRUTH

5

"Now is the time to bring my people together and lead them out of the muddy waters of life." Those were the words the Lord spoke to Rev. Lola Fuller in 1999. She recounts them in an article for Raleigh, North Carolina's *News-Observer*. This message from God propelled Fuller, pastor of Shalom Christian Community Church in Raleigh, to focus her work on the needs of the neighborhood around her church. Rev. Fuller passes out groceries to needy residents and takes prayer walks around the neighborhood, stopping to talk with prostitutes and drug addicts who reside there.

Also in Raleigh, Rev. Minne McCoy serves as associate pastor at Martin Street Baptist Church. She is also executive director for Family Place, an organization that serves the homeless, senior citizens, and disabled people. McCoy explains what Family Place does: "We have a food pantry. We have bank and business professionals that teach (people) how to budget."

Women are often the hearts of African American churches.

For centuries, African American churches have done much more than worship on Sundays. Rev. Vashti McKenzie, a bishop in the African Methodist Episcopal Church, says, "The church has always been the center of the Black community. We have done more than preach the Gospel, we have found ways of going beyond Sunday morning to ministering to people every day." Kelly Starling, writing in *Ebony* magazine, explains: "The Black Church of the 20th century was . . . school, community center, meeting ground, political engine, restorer of hope."

As African American churches have been the hearts of their communities, women have been the hearts of the churches. Charyn D. Sutton reports, "The Black church in America is primarily female in its membership even though the leadership is generally male. Women over 40 form the backbone of most churches."

African American churches today come in all shapes and sizes. Some, like West Angeles Church of God in Christ in West Los Angeles, are huge churches with opulent sanctuaries and state-of-the-art equipment. Others are small congregations of only several dozen members who meet in rented city storefronts. Other African American churches worship in historic countryside wooden chapels.

African American churches may be part of other traditions that have their own chapters in this book: they may be Catholic, Mennonite, Evangelical, or Pentecostal. African American women are also increasingly exploring non-Christian traditions, such as Buddhism.

Some black congregations are part of denominational groups made up almost entirely of African American churches. The African Methodist Episcopal (AME) Church is one such group. Others belong to denominations with churches of various ethnic groups. The American Baptist Church, of which Dr. Martin Luther King Jr. was a member, contains many African American con-

gregations. Recently, new churches have begun to intentionally attract multiracial congregations. Bridgeway Community Church in Columbia, Maryland, a church of more than 1,200, has an African American pastor and members from all different races.

When North American slavery began in Jamestown, Virginia, in 1619, Africans arrived with their own spiritual beliefs and customs. Religious revivals in the 1700s and 1800s brought many blacks—both slaves and freedmen—to a belief in Jesus Christ. Phillis Wheatley, America's first major African American poet, recalls in one of her poems the words of George Whitefield, a white minister who preached to blacks: "Take [Christ], ye Africans, he longs for you . . . you shall be sons, and kings, and priests to God."

White Christians had mixed reactions to the conversion of slaves. Mennonites and Quakers opposed slavery, but unfortunately, such viewpoints were rare in eighteenth- and nineteenth-century North America. In the South, slave owners forced blacks to listen to sermons that justified their mistreatment.

Yet African Americans refused to settle for their owners' version of Christianity. Slaves risked punishment by gathering secretly for their own worship services. In the northern states, where there were many freed slaves, Richard Allen tried to worship alongside whites in a Methodist Church, but he was forced to sit in a separate section. Allen refused to be treated as a second class Christian, and in 1794, he formed the African Methodist Episcopal Church.

Jarena Lee was a member of Richard Allen's church who believed God was calling her to preach. He told her, "Methodists don't permit women preachers." That didn't stop her from proclaiming the Bible in homes, schools, and—when she could get away with it—in churches. She became well known and was

Harriet Tubman

invited to speak all over the northern United States. Seeing her success, Allen finally agreed to let her speak in Methodist churches. In 1833, Lee published the story of her life—the first autobiography by a black woman in the United States.

African American women were instrumental in the struggle for freedom during the nineteeth century. Harriet Tubman, for example, escaped from slavery in 1849, then returned to the South again and again to lead others to freedom. Known as "the Black Moses," she led hundreds to freedom, at great personal risk. Her success in freeing others was due to listening to God's voice, she said; she would pray, and then go where God led her.

Sojourner Truth was born a slave in upstate New York in 1797 and gained freedom in 1827, when slavery was abolished in the state. She received a vision from God, which led her to become a traveling preacher. Crowds in the northern states were influenced by her speeches arguing for the abolition of slavery and for women's equal rights. Her most famous speech was delivered at a woman's rights convention in 1852.

That man over there says a woman needs to be helped into carriages and lifted over ditches. . . . Nobody ever helped me into carriages or over mud puddles. . . . And ain't I a woman? I could work as much and eat as much as a man—when I could get to it—and bear the lash as well and ain't I a woman? I have born 13 children and seen most all sold into slavery and when I cried out a mother's grief none but Jesus heard me . . . and ain't I a woman? That little man in black there say a woman can't have as much rights as a man cause Christ wasn't a woman. Where did your Christ come from? From God and a woman! Man had nothing to do with him!

Sojourner Truth

Throughout the past century, African American women working through their churches have been responsible for many of the advances achieved by people of color in North America. In black communities, the church is not merely a religious organization, separated from the rest of the culture. Instead, the communities revolve around their churches; these churches are schools, social events, sports teams, restaurants, libraries, legal and insurance providers, places for political gatherings, while all the while providing spiritual inspiration to the community as well.

Women in African American churches are honorably referred to as "mother," and pastors' wives are "first ladies" of the church. Women are responsible in large part for all the social, community, and spiritual services that African American churches provide. Women have their own ministry "departments" within the churches, in which they function as evangelists, missionaries, teachers, and choir directors.

Maria K. Frederick, professor of Religion and African American Studies at Harvard and author of *Between Sundays: Black Women and Everyday Struggles of Faith*, explains that African American women have used the challenges they face in society to develop leadership roles apart from men in the church. She says:

> Faith determines what issues they should get involved in. That may be helping a teenage mother pay her bills, changing the linen for the elderly or going to Washington to protest the U.S. Department of Agriculture's treatment of Black farmers.

Despite their strong church involvement, African American women rarely serve as pastors. Nationwide, only 3 percent of black pastors are women. Acceptance of women as church leaders is gaining ground, however, but slowly. In the year 2000, the United Methodist Churches appointed three black clergywomen—Violet Fisher, Linda Lee, and Beverly Shamana—to serve as bishops. (Bishops in the Methodist churches are church leaders in authority over other pastors.) Twelve years before that, Leontine Kelly was appointed in San Francisco, the first African American woman to serve as a Methodist bishop. In 2000, Vashti McKenzie was chosen as the first woman to serve as bishop in the African Methodist Episcopal Church.

As she accepted her new duties, Linda Lee said:

> I will always remember that it was Black clergywomen who gave me encouragement, support and prayers long before this ever occurred. We are here as a testimony that God will carry out God's promises, and I am here to testify that God is faithful.

One area in which African American churchwomen have had tremendous influence—far beyond the Black community—is in music. The popular musi-

African American women have a long and rich tradition within their churches.

cal sounds enjoyed by teenagers of all races in North America today would not be possible without the African American church's heritage of music. African styles of singing were incorporated into the slaves' secret church meetings. Although slave owners banned drums, black congregations retained their African love of percussion by clapping their hands or drumming on logs. "Spiritual" songs were sung during worship and while at work in the fields. These songs expressed what scholars today call "liberation theology." On the surface, a song might be about Moses and the Children of Israel—but the slaves used these Bible stories to express their own hopes for escape and freedom.

The elements of African worship and the "spirituals" of slave days evolved into contemporary popular musical forms. In the 1920s, music from the southern countrysides was taken north into the cities, and sung in "blues" style with guitar and harmonica. Pentecostal churches brought greater energy and more spontaneous arrangements into the mix, along with pianos and brass instruments.

In 1928, a young woman named Mahalia Jackson moved to Chicago, where she washed clothes for a living while singing on the weekends at her Baptist Church. She became popular and eventually world famous—but she insisted on singing only gospel music, and she would not perform in places she regarded as inappropriate for Christians. Nonetheless, she fueled the public's desire for jazz, blues, and gospel music.

Today's gospel music scene is just as sophisticated as the secular hip-hop world, only the lyrics point toward God. The group Trin-i-tee says they "respect excellent music" and incorporate modern beats and rhythms with their gospel recordings. Singer Erica Atkins of the gospel group Mary Mary says, "We serve a big God who doesn't function in a box. Gospel should be where it needs to

be, and that's in the clubs, in the streets, wherever God's message needs to be heard."

Women in today's African American churches continue to fill a wide variety of vital roles. Black churches are thriving in the cities, the suburbs, and the countryside. The "mothers" of the church can be found singing, teaching children how to read, preaching the Word, and serving in a hundred other ways. They continue a long and rich tradition, serving their communities and bringing glory to God.

"A WOMAN OF VALOUR WHO CAN FIND . . . FOR HER PRICE IS FAR
ABOVE RUBIES."
—MISHLEI (PROVERBS) 31:10, JEWISH PUBLICATION SOCIETY OF THE BIBLE

6

WOMEN IN NORTH AMERICAN JUDAISM

"The purpose of clothing is to cover, conceal and obscure—not G-d forbid, the opposite!" These are the words on a sign in the window of a women's clothing store located on Kingston Avenue in Crown Heights, a New York City neighborhood. Another sign reads "Tight clothing emphasizes and draws attention." Most of the people in this neighborhood are Hasidic Jews.

Hasidic law requires women to dress alike, in modest skirts or dresses. Their legs, necks, and elbows cannot be seen in public. Married women keep their hair covered at all times. Until marriage, girls and boys have very little contact with one another. Even when married, men and women do not dance together or mix socially in public. Married women are expected to serve as mothers and keep house. Career women are nonexistent.

Only a few miles away from the store on Kingston Avenue, Alexandra Lebenthal works in her office that looks out over the Statue of Liberty and New York Harbor. Lebenthal, the CEO of Lebenthal and Company, Inc., a

The Jewish faith offers hope and strength to many modern women.

full-service brokerage firm, is featured in a 2002 article in *Jewish Woman* magazine. The business has expanded under her leadership, adding mutual funds, equities, estate planning, insurance, and asset management to its products. In addition to her work as chief executive at the firm, she works with a number of charitable and nonprofit organizations. One of her goals is to see other women advance to head management positions in the New York business world.

Dressed in a business suit, successfully handling a job that would be a challenge to anyone in the city—male or female—it would be hard to imagine anyone more unlike the Hasidic women in Crown heights. Yet the successful business manager in her office and the modestly dressed homemakers on Kingston Avenue share more in common than one might think. They both find strength and meaning in their Jewish faith.

Throughout history, the Jewish people have influenced the world in ways far greater than their numbers. Judaism was the world's first "ethical *monotheism*." In other words, it believes in one God, who holds human beings accountable to live in responsible ways. Without such an idea shaping society, the entire history of Western Civilization would be changed.

The Jewish religion dates from more than a thousand years before the start of the Christian era. Moses, the central figure of Jewish faith, was called by God to liberate Israel from slavery in Egypt. God then gave Moses the Ten Commandments—laws that have guided Western Civilization for thousands of years. God assured Moses his people would inherit a "Promised Land." For more than a thousand years they lived there, then in A.D. 70, the Roman Army destroyed the Jewish nation, and Jews were scattered throughout the earth.

The Jewish people had no homeland for more than 1,800 years. Nevertheless, they kept their ancient language, customs, and beliefs intact, though they suffered persecution in many of the nations where they lived. After the unspeakable horror of the *Holocaust*, Israel was reestablished, a modern Jewish nation in the land God promised to Moses thousands of years before.

Modern Jews debate whether their faith is liberating or oppressive of women. Differing forms of Judaism view women's roles in greatly varying manners. The Hebrew Scriptures provide a number of positive female role models; for example, Moses' sister Miriam was invaluable in assisting Moses to liberate and lead the Israelites from Egypt, and Deborah was the leader of the Israelite tribes, deciding legal matters and even directing warriors in battle. Queen Esther saved Israel from destruction due to her courage and tact. Despite the examples of strong women in the Hebrew Bible, during the years when Jews

Queen Esther provides a role model of a strong and courageous woman leader.

lived among the other nations and were influenced by them, women were given increasingly limited roles in Jewish life.

Judaism in the United States today is divided into four religious movements represented by membership in different types of synagogues. Almost half of all Jews, however, do not belong to any synagogue. These *secular* Jews find a variety of ways to express their Jewish identities. They may attend religious services from time to time, most often on the High Holy Days. Other secular Jews continue on a journey for spiritual truth—sometimes combining elements of their Jewish heritage with ideas from other spiritual traditions.

Orthodox Jews consider themselves the true keepers of Jewish tradition. They believe God gave the entire Torah (law) to Moses in two parts—the written Torah that contains 613 specific laws and the spoken Torah, traditions recorded in writings called the Talmud.

Orthodox teaching emphasizes the dignity and importance of women as wives and mothers. These roles are seen as opportunities for spiritual growth. As one Orthodox writer describes it:

> Home-life in Orthodox Judaism is a rich world of familial love, nurturing of others, prayer, intellect, and communal festivity. One could argue that it is a far more interesting and spiritually satisfying world than the corporate work environment.

Orthodox women are not prohibited from pursuing careers, and they are not condemned if they do not wish to marry. The vast majority of Orthodox women do, however, choose to focus their lives on family rather than education or career.

The *Denver Post* recently reported on Rachel Rabinovitz, an Orthodox Jewish career woman. She is a radiation *oncologist* and clinical researcher who walks to the synagogue on Saturday, follows *kosher* dietary restrictions, and

wears a dark wig to cover her hair, as an Orthodox way to pursue modesty. "I think it's a very possible, desirable and wonderful thing to be able to stay committed to my religion, my tradition, and Orthodox Judaism brings with it a lot of rules," Rabinovitz said. "At the same time, I think I can participate in society. I'm not threatened by it, and I can contribute a lot to it. There is no contradiction."

Orthodox women are traditionally not allowed to read aloud at the synagogue; until recently women were only permitted to read the Torah at all-female prayer groups. Orthodox women are now breaking that mold at mixed gender prayer groups. In New York, Tamara Charm started Darkhei Noam, a prayer group for Orthodox Jewish men and women. Frustrated with the tradition prohibiting women from reading the Torah aloud, she decided to create her own spiritual setting where women and men could both be heard. Praying aloud in a mixed-gender group "makes me feel much more able to connect with God," she says.

The Reform Movement is the largest synagogue group in the United States. Reform Judaism emphasizes *ethics* rather than rituals, and reformed synagogues were the first to ordain women as rabbis. In March of 2003, Rabbi Janet Marder became the first female president of the Reform Movement. Marder is senior rabbi at Congregation Beth Am, a synagogue of more than 1,200 households near San Francisco. She says, "My central goal then and now is to help people discover the beauty and power of our tradition. Our tradition has the power to transform lives. I believe I have been working toward that throughout my career."

Conservative Judaism may be thought of as a sort of "middle ground" between the Orthodox and Reform Synagogues. Conservative Judaism originally

In Orthodox synagogues, women are not allowed to read aloud from the Torah
(except for in all-women prayer groups).

opposed women serving as rabbis, but in recent years that has changed. In February of 2002, Judy Yudof became the first female president of the United Synagogue of Conservative Judaism.

The Reconstructionist Movement is the newest and smallest of the major Jewish groups in the United States. Reconstructionists broke away from Conservative Judaism in the 1920s to follow Rabbi Mordecai Kaplan who believed Judaism needed a complete "reconstruction" for modern times. The Reconstructionist Movement has been the Jewish group most supportive of women's equal rights. For centuries, boys have become Jewish men with a bar mitzvah ceremony in the synagogue—but girls had no corresponding ceremony. The first recorded ceremony of bat mitzvah was held for the daughter of Rabbi Mordecai Kaplan. Women in the Reconstructionist Movement are encouraged to become rabbis.

Hasidic Judaism, the most conservative form of the faith, began as an attempt to restore Judaism to its roots. Powerful spiritual leaders known as rebbes lead it. Hasidic Jews consider the modern world to be evil, and attempt as much as possible to live separated from its influence.

Stephanie Wellen Levine, a Harvard University doctoral candidate and a secular Jew, spent a year in the Crown Heights, Brooklyn, Hasidic community. She followed teenage girls at school, in their homes, and as they socialized, and she published her experiences in a book, Mystics, Mavericks and Merrymakers: An Intimate Journey Among Hasidic Girls. Her book reports that some young women do yearn for the pleasures of secular American life, and some rebel and leave the Hasidic community—but those who do so struggle with the loss of the life they must leave behind. On the whole, Stephanie Levine finds that ultra-Orthodox Jewish teen girls are unusually self-assured and happy. She suggests that living apart from the pressures imposed by boys, dating, and the

problems surrounding teens in the larger society makes Hasidic girls healthier overall.

When one considers the great differences between Reform Judaism on one hand, and Hasidic Jews on the other hand, it is fair to question whether the two are actually the same religion. Yet no matter what beliefs Jews follow, they still share a common history, heritage, language, and culture. The Talmud expresses this by saying, "All Jews are responsible one for another." This is the Jewish value called *Klal Yisrael*, the "Community of Israel."

For three thousand years, Jewish households have celebrated the annual Passover Seder meal. This is a ***commemoration*** of the meal that the Hebrew people ate "in haste," with unleavened bread, the night before they fled from bondage in Egypt. At each Seder meal, an extra cup is set on the table for the prophet Elijah. In the twenty-first century, many Jewish households are adding a second cup—for the prophetess Miriam, Moses' sister. This practice acknowledges the Bible's record that Moses did not achieve liberation alone. It also honors the indispensable contributions made by countless Jewish women through the centuries. The Miriam cup is a recent innovation, yet it is in continuity with three thousand years of tradition—a fitting symbol for Jewish women in America today.

"AND SAY TO THE BELIEVING WOMEN THAT THEY SHOULD . . . GUARD THEIR MODESTY; THAT THEY . . . NOT DISPLAY THEIR BEAUTY EXCEPT TO THEIR HUSBANDS....
—SURAH 24:31, THE HOLY QURAN, TRANSLATED BY ABDULLAH YUSUF ALI.

NORTH AMERICAN MUSLIM WOMEN

"I bear witness that there is no God but Allah, and Mohammed is a prophet of God." When a person says these words with heartfelt conviction, they are regarded as a convert to the religion of Islam. At the start of the twenty-first century, many Americans are making this commitment.

The word Islam means "surrender" or "submit," and to practice Islam is to submit to the will of God. A person who follows this way is a Muslim—in Arabic "one who submits" to God.

Islam is a subject of fascination to many Americans today. On one hand, Muslims are associated with terrorism and Eastern Arab countries. At the same time, Islam is gaining converts and recognition throughout North America. The subject of women's rights in Islam is also much discussed and much misunderstood.

Joanne Richards was born and raised in California, where her teen years were full of trouble. She met a young Muslim man who impressed her as a sin-

Many North American women practice Islam.

cere and spiritual person. That influenced her to read the Quran (the Muslim holy book). She says, "The beauty of its verses galvanized me. What most impressed me was the forgiveness and mercy. That incredible Graciousness of Allah. I was going to need lots of these blessings with the kind of life I was living." She converted to Islam.

Richards admits she hasn't always fit easily into her new faith. "One thing I had a great problem with when I finally accepted that I was becoming Muslim was some of the attitudes of the Muslims I met." Describing her experiences at the mosque, she says, "Usually, the first question is, 'Who is your husband?' If I said that I didn't have one, I was viewed with suspicion and usually no one would talk to me after that." Despite the difficulties, she says, "For me, embracing Islam has been the single greatest gift ever granted to me. I am still grateful and awestruck by it."

America has five to six million followers of Islam. Muslims outnumber Presbyterians, Episcopalians, and Mormons, and they are more numerous than Quakers, Unitarians, Seventh-Day Adventists, Mennonites, Jehovah's Witnesses, and Christian Scientists, combined. Some surveys show Islam has overtaken Judaism as the country's second-most commonly practiced religion. One of the most widespread misconceptions about Muslims in North is that they are primarily Middle Eastern. Fewer than one out of eight American Muslims (12.4 percent) are of Arab descent. The two largest Muslim groups in the United States are native-born African Americans (42 percent) and immigrants from South Asia (24 percent). An increasing number of converts also come from mainstream American culture. When Mariam Agah (formerly Mary Froelich) started questioning her Catholic faith, she was not only white and middle class—she was a nun. At the age of twenty-five, she left her religious order and then proceeded to read her way through many bookshelves of

philosophy. Two works stood out: the Koran and the *Autobiography of Malcolm X*. "I continued my spiritual journey," she says, "and it led me to Islam."

The Prophet Mohammed was born in A.D. 571 in Mecca, in Arabia. At the age of forty, he received supernatural revelations that showed him the way of submission to Allah. (Allah is the Arabic word meaning "God," and Jews and Christians in Arabic-speaking countries use the same word to describe God in their faiths as well.) Mohammed's revelations were written down and collected in the book called the Quran. After the Prophet's death, Islam split into two branches, Sunnis and Shiites. Their beliefs are similar, but Shiites invest more authority in their Imams (spiritual leaders).

Submission to God (Allah) involves five essential spiritual practices, which are known as the "five pillars" of Islam:

1. the declaration of faith, to "testify that there is no deity except God, and that Muhammad is His Messenger"
2. to pray five times a day
3. to pay the yearly *alms*
4. to fast during the month of Ramadan
5. to make the pilgrimage to Mecca

Women are oppressed in some of the Islamic nations, but scholars of the Quran in America insist the Holy Book itself does not sanction such oppression. Tasleem Griffin in an article on the "Why Islam" Web site says, "In a time when most women were common *chattel*, the teachings of the Quran and the practices firmly restored to them status, both legal and social; and dignity as individuals." Griffin goes on to explain, "Not one verse in the whole of the Quran speaks injustice. Not one word says, men and women are not equal."

Though men and women are equal in Islam, their roles are not the same.

The need of woman, in child bearing years is sustenance and security. A pregnant woman requires care; a nursing mother and infant require protection; a wife, mother, sister require respect: these are their rights.

The Quran states men are the stronger sex, and protectors of women.

> Men are the protectors and maintainers of women, because Allah has made one of them stronger than the other, and because they spend out of their possessions [to support them]. (Quran 4:34)

In the economy of the home, the Quran says, "men have a degree of advantage above them [women]" (Quran 2:228).

The covering of women's heads is an issue that generates considerable discussion both within and without Islam. Laila Al-Marayati and Semeen Issa recently sent this anecdote to the *Los Angeles Times*:

> A few years ago, someone from the Feminist Majority Foundation called the Muslim Women's League to ask if she could "borrow a *burka*" for a photo shoot the organization was doing to draw attention to the plight of women in Afghanistan under the Taliban. When we told her that we didn't have one, and that none of our Afghan friends did either, she expressed surprise, as if she'd assumed that all Muslim women keep burkas in their closets in case a militant Islamist comes to dinner. She didn't seem to understand that her assumption was the equivalent of assuming that every Latino has a Mexican sombrero in their closet.

The Quran most certainly does not require a full covering of the face (like the Afghan burka) but there is controversy whether the Quran requires a scarf over the hair (Hijab). Quran 24:31 says women must "guard their modesty" and therefore they should "draw their veils over their bosoms." This verse is vari-

ously interpreted. Some say that a veil over the head is assumed by the verse, others claim that only covering of the chest is required.

Many Muslim women, both in America and in progressive Muslim nations like Jordan, choose not to wear the hijab. An article posted by the Muslim Women's League states:

> The scarf, an article of clothing, has sadly become a litmus test for a Muslim woman's faith and devotion to God. Ultimately, what really matters is the attitude, behavior and demeanor of the person in question.

At the same time, for many American Muslims the veil is important for their spiritual identity. Mohja Kahf, professor of English at the University of Arkansas, says, "I believe hijab is pleasing to Allah, or I wouldn't wear it. I believe there is something deep down beautiful and dignified about it. It has brought some beautiful and joyous dimension to my life that always amazes me." Fariha Khan, a teen in Rockville, Maryland, says, "To me hijab is a gift from Allah. It gives me the opportunity to become closer to Allah. Also quite importantly, [it provides me] the chance to stand and be recognized as a Muslim."

While there is widespread agreement that the Quran does not itself discriminate against women, Muslim women in America do nonetheless face certain challenges because of their faith. On the one hand, the non-Muslim American public discriminate against them and misunderstand them.

When Samer Hathout, a Muslim woman who works as a prosecuting attorney in Los Angeles, addressed a U.N. assembly with a speech about challenges facing American Muslim women, she said:

> As a minority in the United States, Muslims face many challenges. First and foremost is ignorance about Islam. This ignorance leads to stereotyp-

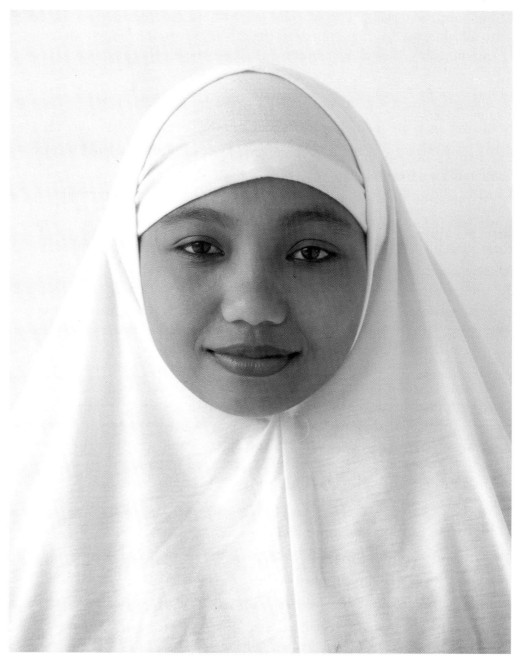

Many Muslim women choose to wear a head covering, while others do not.

ing, fear, and distrust. The acts of a few Muslim *extremists* are attributed to all Muslims. Muslim American citizens' loyalty to the United States is questioned. We are *dehumanized* and thus easy prey for prejudice.

She goes on to say, "a woman who wears hijab, which is the traditional headcovering, is often taunted at work and on the street, and the careers of a lot of these women are actually jeopardized—they are discriminated against at work and they are not given jobs."

At the same time, some Muslim women face sexist attitudes and actions from their fellow believers. Although the Quran assures them of fair treatment, there are still Muslim men in America who have migrated from countries where the culture is disparaging of women. Hathout goes on to say:

Muslim women often face discrimination from their own Muslim community. Discrimination by Muslims primarily results from ignorance about Islam and the importation of cultural attitudes that demean women. Islam is often interpreted in ways that are sexist and not true to the true teachings of equality in the Quran. [The teachings of Prophet Muhammad] are taken out of context and used to justify certain behavior. . . . Some of the most serious problems that we American Muslim women face include: domestic violence, abuse of divorce and child custody laws, abuse of the polygamy system, and isolation and exclusion from various aspects of Muslim life.

Of course, Muslim women are not alone in having problems of this sort, and many female followers of Islam find satisfaction in their faith. Karla, a blond-haired, blue-eyed, American-born convert to Islam, explains her choice: "The main question people seem to ask, is 'How could you, an educated American woman convert to Islam—a religion that oppresses women?'" She tells them

the Quran supports women's rights, though some misinterpret it. "I had a choice—deny what I believe [that Mohammed is a Prophet of God] . . . or accept what I believe, but work to change the problems that exist within the Muslim community. I chose the latter."

"[I AM] UTTERLY FREE FROM ALL SORROW, A DOER OF THE
BUDDHA'S TEACHINGS."
— FROM KERIGATHA, A POEM BY KHEMA, AN ENLIGHTENED
NUN WHO RECEIVED TEACHING FROM SHAKYAMUNI BUDDHA

NORTH AMERICAN BUDDHIST WOMEN

Catharine Burroughs seems in many respects like other women in North America. She was born and raised in Brooklyn, likes to have her nails done, wears a black leather jacket, and she enjoys shopping, listening to Motown, music and watching *Star Trek*. Yet her pursuit of a spiritual life has given her a new name—Jetsunma Ahkon Lhamo—and an important spiritual role—she is a Lama, a revered teacher of Tibetan Buddhism.

In 1985, she was a Maryland housewife with two children. A prayer group met in her basement, and an Indian monastery contacted Burroughs and asked if she would host His Holiness Penor Rinpoche, one of the most important lamas of Tibetan Buddhism, when he visited America. After meeting Burroughs, His Holiness recognized her as being capable of experiencing an unusual degree of spiritual illumination. In 1988, Rinpoche declared her to be a *tulku*, or **reincarnated** teacher.

The historical Buddha is seen by his followers as a human
being who was totally awake to spiritual reality.

Since that time, Jetsunma has established Kunzang Palyul Chöling, (KPC) Tibetan Buddhist centers that function under her guidance. Members of KPC say one of their most important endeavors is a twenty-four-hour prayer vigil for peace that has gone unbroken for sixteen years. The lofty spiritual goals of KPC can be seen in its membership vows: "Taking no thought for my comfort or safely, precious Lama, make of me a pure and perfect instrument by which the end of suffering and death in all forms might be realized."

Jetsunma Ahkon Lhamo is unusual in having attained such a high rank within Tibetan Buddhism. Traditionally, leaders have been male. It is not unusual, however, for women in North America to practice the Buddhist faith in its various forms, although it is difficult to come up with a count of how many people in the United States and Canada are practicing Buddhists; estimates vary between 2 and 4 million.

The word "Buddha" means "awakened one." It refers to a person who has achieved spiritual illumination. All persons are potential buddhas. The historical figure commonly referred to as *the* Buddha was born in 566 B.C. in what is today southern Nepal. His family name was Guatama, and his personal name was Siddhartha. He is not regarded by his followers as a god, or a special form of spiritual being, or a prophet. Instead, he was a human being like others who one day woke up to the fullness of spiritual reality.

In May of 531 B.C., Siddhartha sat beneath a fig tree in deep meditation. As he did so, he attained an extraordinary state of enlightenment, or spiritual knowledge. He said, "Now the bonds of ignorance and craving are sundered, deliverance is obtained for all! All living beings are buddhas, endowed with wisdom and virtue!" He now possessed the "Dharma," or teachings that would define Buddhism for centuries thereafter. The Dharma can be summarized by four noble truths:

1. All life is suffering
2. The cause of suffering is desire.
3. Suffering can be ended.
4. The way to end suffering is the Noble Eightfold Path.

The Noble Eightfold path consists of the following:

1. right understanding
2. right thought
3. right speech
4. right action
5. right livelihood
6. right effort
7. right mindfulness
8. right meditation

In the centuries following Guatama Buddha's life, those who followed the Dharma separated into three distinct traditions: Theravada, Mahayana, and Vajrayna. The rituals and emphases of each group differ, but they share the same basic beliefs.

Buddhists practice meditation, compassion, and student-mentor relationships in order to grow in enlightenment. Meditation has become enormously popular in America over the past decade, and is practiced for health benefits by many who do not consider themselves Buddhist as well as those who do. Buddhist meditation involves "stilling" oneself physically, mentally, and emotionally. By freeing the mind, one is able to get in touch with the truth.

Buddhism's most important ethical concept is, "Avoid causing harm to other *sentient* beings." In North American Buddhism, women have proven to be teachers and models of compassion.

Yeshe Wangmo was born in 1949 in Montreal, Canada, where as an adult, she worked as a sociologist in the field of mental health. She says:

> I remember, a long time ago when I was living in Guatemala in a very idyllic situation where I had everything that I wanted in the world, I was completely fulfilled, until one day I realized that this is great but it's really only benefiting me. And that's when I knew that life was not about making myself comfortable and satisfying my desires, but that I also had a desire, not only a desire, but there is really something important in the sharing between beings. I really believe that all beings are meant to live together in their interconnectedness. . . . So with that idea I left that place and shortly thereafter went into looking for a spiritual path.

In 1978, she met two famous Tibetan masters who inspired her to follow their path, and in 1992, she was enthroned as a Lama.

One way Wangmo serves as a spiritual teacher is by visiting with prisoners on death row. Her view that each life is just one of many in succession helps her to deal compassionately with the things that death row prisoners have done. She says, "People always have positive qualities, even while they're so-called criminals." She says of one man, whom she befriended on death row, "He was a perfect criminal, and he was a perfect Buddha. And so he was also a perfect example." She concludes:

> Actually everyone without exception, on death row, or off death row, is a source of inspiration for me. I realized that if a death row person can be my teacher, so can my neighbor next door. All it takes is the time and the ability to connect with people.

Along with the practices of meditation and compassion, Buddhists enter into a teacher-student relationship to follow the Dharma. Whereas Christianity, Judaism, and Islam are religions of "the book," Buddhism places much greater emphasis on what can be experienced in relationship with a living master. Collections of sacred texts exist, but these cannot in themselves communicate the way.

Historically, Buddhists have not given women the same stature as men in the practice of their religion. Jack Maguire, in *Essential Buddhism*, writes:

> Like the other major world religions . . . Buddhism evolved in a ***patriarchal*** society and inevitably took on some of the same bias. Even the Buddha was compelled to a certain degree to be a man of the time in this regard. He therefore originally restricted membership in his Sangha [school] to men.

Since his mother had died while Siddhartha was young, his aunt Prajapti raised him. At the time when Buddha received enlightenment, Prajapti was already highly regarded as a queen and a powerful leader. She repeatedly asked Siddhartha to allow women to form an order of nuns and follow his Dharma. He gave in and granted her wish.

As Sandy Boucher, a Buddhist and feminist living in Oakland California, says:

> Buddhism has traditionally been a male-dominated religion. That characteristic extends both to most temples or centers in Asia and to those founded by Asian immigrants, which tend to be headed by male teachers. Women have played a major role, however, in North American Buddhism—which has become much more respectful of women's equality.

Boucher reflects on the progress women have made in American Buddhism. "Already in our young American Buddhism, we have seen a tradition of strong women teachers. There have been several 'generations' of female teachers, and it is possible to find and study with most of these women now."

Writing in the *Miami Herald*, Aileen Dodd tells about Ani Karma Chtso, "a former Protestant who sang in the church choir and picked wheat on her family's North Dakota farm." She now runs Kagyu Shedrup Chling Tibetan Buddhist Dharma Center in Hollywood, Florida. Chtso says:

I was very much a feminist. Very vocal and very loud. I was a little concerned when I learned about the history and that in places like Tibet, men were the only people trained in Buddhism. I went to my lama and asked him about it and he said it is very easy to look from the outside and criticize. The only way you can change something is to be part of it and change it from the inside. In America, I think the women's movement has done wonders.

Once viewed as a religion for Asians, American Buddhism is becoming increasingly diverse. More and more African Americans are attracted to its teachings. Examples are Tina Turner, who speaks of her Buddhism in her autobiography, and Alice Walker, who described herself as a Buddhist practitioner in a year 2000 *New York Times* article. Black female Buddhists see connection between the powerful social movements in the African American community and the social compassion taught in Buddhism. The year before he was assassinated, Dr. Martin Luther King Jr. nominated Vietnamese Buddhist monk Thich Nhat Hanh for the Nobel Peace Price. African American professor and author bell hooks tells about her experience meeting Hanh:

Alice Walker

He embraced me as a fellow teacher, not as if "Oh, you're coming to bow down to me." He had no difficulty giving me that expansive sense of "Your work has been doing the work of Dharma, and I see that."

In June of 2000, American Buddhists experienced a rare treat when 220 North American Buddhist teachers gathered in Marin County, California, to speak with the most revered figure of world Buddhism—the Dalai Lama. More than half of those gathered were women. His Holiness was asked if he believed there could be a female Dalai Lama in the future, and he admitted the possibility. Few people expect that to happen soon—Tibetan Buddhism is still far more conservative than its American counterpart.

bell hooks

Yet North American women are bringing changes to this 2,500-year-old faith, and no one knows where it might evolve. Guatama Buddha said his teachings were like rain; they bear fruit that differs according to the seed itself. The world is only beginning to see what will grow from the Buddha's words as they awaken more and more seeds in the minds of North America's Buddhist women.

"DO YE MEN SHOW THEM HONOUR. THE RIGHTEOUSNESS OF MEN DEPENDS
UPON WOMEN. ALL PLEASURES AND ENJOYMENTS ALSO COMPLETELY DEPEND
UPON THEM. DO YE SERVE THEM AND WORSHIP THEM. DO YE BEND YOUR
WILLS BEFORE THEM."
—ANUSASANA PARVA, SECTION XLVI.

9

NORTH AMERICAN HINDU WOMEN

"I am a Hindu who flipped burgers for a living all through college." So writes Shoba Narayan, in Beliefnet. She explains, "I had grown up in a devout Hindu household in India, but when I came to America to attend Mount Holyoke College . . . I needed money. While interviewing for the job, I didn't tell my supervisor that not only was I a vegetarian who had never eaten a burger in my life but that eating beef was against my religion."

She wore gloves so she didn't have to touch the meat, and sometimes covered her face with a mask to deal with the smell. She didn't tell her parents that she worked with meat. If her mother had known, "She would have demanded that I return to India immediately and hold elaborate purification ceremonies to rid me of my bad *karma*." It may seem odd to work with hamburgers and never taste one, but as Narayan says, "As an immigrant Hindu, my life is full of such *paradoxes*."

It is estimated that at least 250,000 Hindus live in Canada, and more than 1.5 million live in America. That makes Hinduism North America's fifth largest religion. Unlike other religions in this book, however, there have been relatively few converts to Hinduism in America. The Society for Krishna Consciousness, which became popular during the 1960s, has less than 3,000 members. Instead, most American Hindus are immigrants or the children of immigrants from India and other Eastern countries.

Unlike Christianity and other Western religions, Hinduism does not trace back to an important founding person and does not have a central religious organization. Instead, it consists of many different religious beliefs, originating in India over 4,000 years ago. Hinduism recognizes a single deity, but also recognizes other gods and goddesses as forms or aspects of that supreme God.

Hinduism is very tolerant of other religions. There is a saying: "The truth is One, but different Sages call it by Different Names."

Hindu Scriptures include the Vedas, Upanishads, and the Mahabarata. The Bhagavad Gita (part of the Mahabarata) is perhaps the most popular sacred text in Hinduism. The Gita is a discussion between the warrior Arjuna and the god Krishna. Arjuna is about to enter an important battle, but he suddenly decides that it is better to refuse to fight and adopt Ahimsa, the principle of non-violence.

Hindus believe in reincarnation, where the soul transfers after death into another body. During each life, a person accumulates karma, the sum of good and bad deeds. How you will live your next life is determined by your karma. If you live with pure acts, you will be reborn into a higher form of life. Bad deeds can cause you to be reborn as a lower level, or even as an animal. Whether or not a person has wealth, honor, or good fortune is seen as the consequences of good or bad karma, earned during previous lives.

WOMEN IN NORTH AMERICA'S RELIGIOUS WORLD

When Westerners discuss Hinduism, they often refer to "sacred cows." In fact, cows are not regarded as "sacred" in the sense that they are to be worshiped. They are, however, highly respected. Hindus regard not only cattle but also all living creatures as sacred. To the Hindu, the cow symbolizes all other creatures. The cow gives and sustains life.

The cow symbolizes to Hindus the sacredness of all living creatures.

Hindu men as well as women traditionally wear a dot on the forehead, though the practice is uncommon now with men. The dot has a mystical meaning, for it represents the Third Eye or spiritual sight that Hindus seek to awaken through *yoga*. An unmarried girl wears a black dot, and a married girl a red one.

The dot on this woman's forehead represents the "Third Eye"—the spiritual sight that Hindus seek to achieve.

Traditional Indian styles have become popular recently in American women's fashions. Rama Mulukutla, a college student of Indian heritage, says, "Imagine a culture where women are adorned with beautiful, jeweled bhindis on their foreheads and display nose rings, toe rings, delicate silver anklets, and henna body paints." She then points out that ornamentation that is "very sacred to Indian women" has become "mainstream fashion trends" in America. She recalls how she was made fun of when wearing such items as a child, when they were symbols of her heritage but were not yet accepted in North American culture. Seeing how what was formerly strange is now a fashion fad, she hopes "we can learn to respect other cultures and traditions, no matter how foreign they may seem to us."

Traditionally, women's roles in Hinduism have been rather narrow, compared to modern Western ideals. "Women have one eternal duty in this world, dependence upon and obedient service to their husbands, and this one duty constitutes their only end," states the Mahabharata Anusasana Parva, Section LIX. At the same time, the religious text also says:

Do ye men show them honour. The righteousness of men depends upon women. All pleasures and enjoyments also completely depend upon them. Do ye serve them and worship them. Do ye bend your wills before them. (Anusasana Parva, Section XLVI)

Westerners have pointed fingers at the mistreatment of women in India. Sati, the sacrifice of wives upon their husbands' deaths, is an especially awful example. Hindu scholars are quick to reply that such practices are cultural rather than religious. Nothing in the Hindu spiritual tradition requires or supports such actions. The abuse of wives by their husbands is statistically as prevalent in the West as it is in the East.

Hinduism offers worshipers female goddesses as well as male.

Compared to Christianity, Islam, or Judaism, Hinduism places greater emphasis on female aspects of the divine. Hinduism contains female goddesses like Kali, Durga, Lakshmi, and Sarasvati. These represent various feminine qualities of the Divine Being. Hinduism also has deities that are both male and female, so masculine forms of the divine also have their feminine counterparts. Sanatana Dharma, Hinduism's universal tradition, recognizes that the divine contains both masculine and feminine attributes. Hinduism suggests that without recognizing the feminine aspect of divinity one cannot claim to know God.

Traditionally, parents have arranged Hindu marriages. Many modern American Hindus still follow this custom, at least in part. A *Prism Online* article by Miguel Helft tells of a couple, Rajiv and Vandana, whose parents were instrumental in arranging their marriage. Rajiv had been living in the United States and one day told his parents he wished to marry. "He asked them to find a young woman who was raised in an Indian city, spoke English, was willing to live in the United States, and looked good." At the same time, in India, Vandana had finished college and her parents were seeking a mate for their daughter. They suggested several possible husband whom she disliked. Then they came across Rajiv. The couple exchanged pictures and resumes and spoke on the phone. They each wanted to make sure the other was not being forced into this marriage. Not too long after, they were happily wedded.

Chitra Banerjee Divakaruni, who grew up in India and moved to America when she was nineteen, has written a collection of short stories titled *Arranged Marriage*. She met and chose her own husbands, then spent six months convincing her mother to accept him. Now she sees value in both traditional and new ways:

Some Hindu deities have both male and female characteristics.

Arranged marriages come from a different concept of the family. You trust the wisdom of older relatives. Ideally, they make good decisions for you and the rest of the family. Here we are so used to making our own decisions and arranged marriage sounds so strange.

Each year, more than 100,000 Hindu students come to study at colleges in the United States and Canada. Like students of other faiths, they often drift away from practicing their religion. At the same time, many other Hindu students choose to deepen their spirituality and share it with others as well. The Hindu Students Council, an organization that promotes understanding of Hindu culture and heritage, has fifty-six college chapters and five high school chapters across the United States and Canada.

While Indian immigrants find themselves influenced by the customs of broader North American culture, the United States and Canada have in turn been influenced by Indian spirituality. In 1893, Swami Vivekananda introduced Americans to Hinduism when he came to Chicago. More recently, the *Chicago Tribune* reported on Chalanda Sai Ma's visit to the same city. Her visit is "the latest appearance of a growing number of women spiritual guides either from India or claiming wisdom gained there. Called 'divine mothers' by their followers, they are a new, female face of an old tradition: the guru abroad in the United States." Spiritual seekers, some of whom flew along to hear more of her teachings on a six-city tour through America, eagerly received her words.

The Hindu religion is a relative newcomer to this continent. The majority of Hindus in the United States and Canada are still first or second generation. That's a very short time, especially since this is one of the most ancient religions in the world. Devotees would say karma will take many lifetimes to reach its goals. Already, however, North American cultural values are changing the ways Hindu women live out their faith, and Hindu practices are in turn making their mark on the lives of women in the United States and Canada.

"I AM THE GRACIOUS GODDESS WHO GIVES THE GIFT OF JOY UNTO THE
HEART OF MAN.
BEHOLD, I AM THE MOTHER OF ALL THINGS; AND MY LOVE IS POURED
OUT UPON EARTH."
— FROM THE "CHARGE OF THE GODDESS,"
A TEXT READ AT WICCAN INITIATIONS, WRITTEN BY DOREEN VALIENTE

10

NORTH AMERICAN WOMEN WHO PRACTICE WICCA AND NEOPAGANISM

"Mom, Dad, I have something to tell you." The eighteen-year-old college student sat on the couch, nervously twining her fingers and moving her gaze from the floor to her parents' faces. A few moments of awkward silence followed.

Her mother finally spoke in a quavering voice. "Are you wanting to tell us you're a lesbian? If you are, we want you to know. . ."

"Oh, gosh—no, Mom! And I'm not pregnant either. Just let me say what I have to say!"

Her parents waited.

She reached down to her neck and pulled on a silver chain, then took in her fingers a silver brooch with a fancy knot-work pattern resembling a five-pointed star. She stared at it momentarily, as if gathering courage from this talisman, then said, "I've changed my religion. It's important to me, what I believe now, and I want you to understand it." She paused a moment, then went on. "I'm practicing Wicca."

This took a moment to sink in, but then her parents' questions came quickly.
"You mean you're a witch?"

"Some of us call ourselves that—but we don't use that word very much, because it is so often misunderstood."

"Do you worship the devil? What will people at our church say?"

"They can say what they want to, but I don't worship the devil. I don't even believe in a devil. I worship the Goddess."

Wicca, which is the most common form of a broader movement known as Neopaganism, may be North America's fastest growing religion. Like the young woman in the preceding paragraphs, many people who practice Wicca are hesitant to tell others—even friends and family—because they fear misunderstanding. Some witches prefer to stay, as they put it, "in the broom closet." Estimates of Wiccan numbers vary greatly, from a low guess of 200,000 to the high guess of 5 million in North America today. A recent attempt to determine

Wicca offers women a spiritual practice that empowers females.

numbers based on results of the American Religious Identification Survey came up with an estimated 750,000 practitioners in the United States, and 40,000 in Canada. Those numbers would make Wicca the seventh largest religion in North America. Whatever the number, all religious scholars agree: Wicca is growing very quickly.

Young women are the most common converts to Wiccan belief. One reason for this is women's desire for a religion that elevates women. Wicca and other forms of Neopaganism are unique in the way they elevate the worship of female deities. Recent trends in popular entertainment have also popularized witchcraft. Catherine Edwards, in an article in the *Washington Times* newspaper, writes:

> In the last five years Hollywood has produced films including *Practical Magic* and *The Craft* celebrating such cults and featuring hip actresses Nicole Kidman, Sandra Bullock and *Party of Five's* Neve Campbell as witches. Primetime TV has cashed in with its own witchy programming. *Sabrina the Teenage Witch*, *Buffy the Vampire Slayer*, and *Charmed* all feature young females with magical powers. Felicity, on the program of the same, has a Wiccan roommate.

The word "wicca" (pronounced "wik-ah") is an ancient Anglo Saxon term and root for the common word "witch." Gerald Gardner, the founder of modern-day witchcraft, popularized the word in the 1950s. A person who practices witchcraft is a "Wiccan." Wicca is a specific form of a broader set of beliefs known as Neopaganism, or simply Paganism, which is the worship of goddesses and gods, as opposed to the single God of Christianity, Judaism, and Islam.

The "neo" attached to Neopaganism, indicates that these beliefs are attempting to restart ancient traditions that ended, or came close to ending, in centuries past. Forms of Paganism distinct from witchcraft include Druidism (the worship of ancient Celtic deities), Asatru (worship of the ancient Norse deities), Egyptian

Ancient Pagans worshipped aspects of Nature.

Neopaganism, Greco-Roman Paganism, the Women's Spirituality Movement, Unitarian Universalist Pagans (affiliated with churches of that name), and a great variety of others. Its followers often refer to Wicca as "the Craft."

Most modern pagans claim some connection between their beliefs and the religions of people in very ancient times. Stone Age people did worship the Goddess, as proven by archaeology. It is unclear, however, whether there is real continuity between these ancient beliefs and the Craft of today. Ancient Paganism centered on blood sacrifices—either animal or human—and blood sacrifices play no role in today's Wiccan rituals. Ritual prostitution was also a common element in ancient Paganism, and it too is no longer practiced today.

James Lewis writes in *Witchcraft Today: An Encyclopedia of Wiccan and Neopagan Traditions:*

> Much of the appeal of the modern Neopagan Witchcraft movement has been its claim that it embodies an ancient lineage dating back to the pre-Christian religions of Europe. However, as a number of recent investigations have decisively demonstrated, Wicca was founded in the twentieth century by Gerald Gardner, a retired British civil servant.

Many features of today's witchcraft, such as the common Wiccan greeting ("Blessed Be"), the Threefold Law of Return (described below), uses of the Athame (sacred knife) and the Book of Shadows (the book of spells used by each particular group of witches) are all Gardner's contributions.

The Goddess is the central figure and very essence of Neopagan Witchcraft. She is known as the Great Mother, as Mother Nature, as the Queen of Heaven, and as the Moon. Wicca recognizes both female and male qualities within the Divine Force. The male principle is revered as the Horned God, but often excluded or deemphasized in comparison with the Goddess.

The practice of Magick is the element of contemporary witchcraft that most resembles popular caricatures of the Craft. The spelling of "magick" with a "k" is used to distinguish it from the "magic" used by stage illusionists such as David Copperfield. Aleister Crowley, another pioneer of modern witchcraft, defined magick as "the ability to make changes in physical reality by nonphysical means, especially by sheer willpower." Working of Magick usually involves use of ritual objects such as a magic circle, a sacred knife (Athame), a wand, or symbols of the four elements—fire, air, water, and earth. The Goddess or other deities are called upon. Chanting, dancing, and sex may also be involved.

Wiccans believe magick is governed by the "Threefold Law of Return," which states that any magick worked upon others will return to its originator three times as strongly. This is strong motivation to only cast positive spells.

Wiccans and other Neopagans adamantly deny any connection with Satanism. Satanism—the worship of the Christian devil—does take place in North America, as evidenced by mutilated animal remains left in cemeteries and vandalism directed against Christian churches. At the present time, however, no large organized

A female image of the divine force.

Satanist movement or group is known to exist. Dana Corby, writing in the Witches' Voice Web site, says:

> Just like Christian parents, we are especially concerned about literature which links Witchcraft and satanism. We agree with them that satanism is not anything we want our children involved in; we just adamantly contend that it has nothing to do with us.

It should also be noted that there are no actual ties between the enormously popular Harry Potter books and Neopagan Witchcraft. Dana Corby goes on to say that Harry Potter is "a charming fantasy and a great read" but, "(1) it does not even vaguely resemble real magic, (2) it does not encourage (much less teach) witchcraft or sorcery, and (3) it has nothing to do with satanism. And by the way, (4) neither do we."

Neopagan Witchcraft is appealing for women seeking an empowering religion. Worship of the Goddess honors various stages of women's lives—virgin, mother, and elderly sage (crone). Women's wisdom and spiritual power are celebrated. The Goddess is also associated with the renewing strength of nature, appealing to persons who are concerned with *ecology*.

In 1971, Zsusanna Budapest founded a coven (congregation of witches) in Los Angeles, California, which she called "the Susan B. Anthony Coven"—named after the leader of the women's *suffrage* movement. This new and very successful coven admitted only women. Budapest also published a book, *The Feminist Book of Light and Shadows*, which eliminates male references from the *Book of Shadows* commonly used by other covens.

Starhawk, the best known spokesperson for Wicca today, is a student of Budapest. She founded Reclaiming, A Center for Feminist Spirituality and

Counseling, in Berkeley, California. She has served as director, teacher, and counselor at the center, which offers classes, workshops, rituals, and private counseling in the Goddess religion. Her own description of her first book, *Spiral Dance*, summarizes Starhawk's beliefs. She says it is

> an overview of the growth, suppression, and modern-day reemergence of the Old Religion of the Goddess, the pre-Christian tradition known as Paganism, Wicca, or Witchcraft. The book presents the history, philosophy, theology and practice of this serious and much misunderstood religion, and explores its growing influence on the feminist and ecology movements.

Only one moral principle exists in Neopagan Witchcraft; the "Wiccan Rede." The Rede (Old English word for "counsel") says, "If it harms none, do as you will." As James Lewis points out, "Some feel that this is too slender a 'rede' on which to base an ethic adequate for a religious movement as large as Neopaganism." Since Wiccans deny any system defining right and wrong, how can they be sure of what "harms" or does not harm others? Psychologist and Wiccan priestess Vivianne Crowley says, "In the circle, there are no absolutes—no rights and wrongs." This fits with the belief that each person is herself a form of the Goddess. Phillip Davis, Professor of Religion at the University of Prince Edward Island in Canada, says, "Encouraging people to think they are divine is very dangerous—it takes the limits off and doesn't leave any moral restraints."

Wicca's moral openness can be appealing for teens that are fed up with rules. Says one high school practitioner, "Wicca allows me to create my own religion and that suits me." Yet the flexibility of Neopagan Witchcraft may also be a liability. In every religion, unbalanced people may use spirituality as a way to vic-

Starhawk

timize others. A religion that is practiced in secret and follows very few moral guidelines has the potential to be dangerous.

The Witches' Voice Web site instructs minors wanting to learn witchcraft to do so only with the clear approval of their parents. "If your parents are still dead-set against it, you will just have to be patient." It also cautions, "Never be alone with an adult teacher." The same site says if someone offers to teach you witchcraft on the Internet, tell your parents before you begin a correspondence. "If you can't tell them, do not try to sneak around. Do not try to hide e-mail correspondence. If your parents find it one day, not only may you be in trouble, but you may have caused problems for someone else as well."

For some, Wicca is the wonderful reinvention of an ancient faith that gives women power and honor denied to them in other religions. Its harsher critics see Wicca as a trendy spiritual excuse to do whatever feels good. Whether or not you believe in magick, what's certain is that witches are going to play an increasingly important role as women in North America's religious scene.

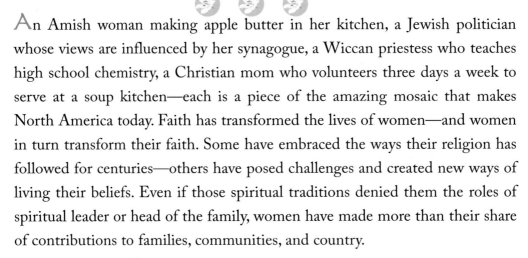

An Amish woman making apple butter in her kitchen, a Jewish politician whose views are influenced by her synagogue, a Wiccan priestess who teaches high school chemistry, a Christian mom who volunteers three days a week to serve at a soup kitchen—each is a piece of the amazing mosaic that makes North America today. Faith has transformed the lives of women—and women in turn transform their faith. Some have embraced the ways their religion has followed for centuries—others have posed challenges and created new ways of living their beliefs. Even if those spiritual traditions denied them the roles of spiritual leader or head of the family, women have made more than their share of contributions to families, communities, and country.

FURTHER READING

Eknath, Easwaran (translator). *The Bhagavad Gita.* New York: Random House, 2000.

Epstein, Daniel Mark. *Sister Aimee: the Life of Aimee Semple McPherson.* Orlando, Fla.: Harvest Books, 1994.

Evans, Mary J. and Kroeger, Clark, Catherine. *The IVP Women's Bible Commentary.* Downers Grove, Ill.: Intervarsity Press, 2002.

Grady, J. Lee. *10 Lies the Church Tells Women: How the Bible has been Misused to Keep Women in Spiritual Bondage.* Lake Mary, Fla.: Charisma House, 2000.

The Holy Bible: New Revised Standard Version. Nashville, Tenn.: Thomas Nelson Publishers, 1989.

Kaylin, Lucy. *For the Love of God: the Faith and the Future of the American Nun.* New York: Harper Collins, 2000.

Laake, Deborah. *Secret Ceremonies: A Mormon Woman's Intimate Diary of Marriage and Beyond.* New York: William Morrow, 1994.

Lewis, James R. *Witchcraft Today: An Encyclopedia of Wiccan and Neopagan Traditions*. Santa Barbara, Calif.: ABC-CLIO, 1999.

Liefeld, Walter, and Tucker, Ruth. *Daughters of the Church: Women and Ministry from New Testament Times to the Present*. Grand Rapids, Mich.: Acadamie Books, 1987.

Maguire, Jack. *Essential Buddhism: A Complete Guide to Beliefs and Practices*. New York: Pocket Books, 2001.

Smith, Joseph (translator). *The Book of Mormon: Another Testament of Jesus Christ*. Salt Lake City, Utah: Church of Jesus Christ of Latter Day Saints, 1981.

Stoltzfus, Louise. *Amish Women: Lives and Stories*. Intercourse, PA: Good Books, 1986.

Williams, Peter J. *America's Religions: Traditions and Cultures*. New York: Macmillan, 1990.

Yusuf, Abdullah Ali. *The Meaning of the Holy Quran*. Beltsville, Mass.: Amana Publications, 1989.

FOR MORE INFORMATION

Christians for Biblical Equality
www.cbeinternational.org

The Church of Jesus Christ of Latter Day Saints
www.mormon.org

Mennonite Central Committee Women's Concerns
www.mcc.org/us/womensconcerns

Black and Christian: A Voice for the African-American Church Community
www.blackandchristian.com

Jewish Women International
www.jwmag.org

Muslim Women's League
www.mwlusa.org

Women Active in Buddhism
members.tripod.com/~lhamo/index.htm

Hinduism Online
www.himalayanacademy.com

The Witches' Voice
www.witchvox.com

Publisher's note:
The Web sites listed on these pages were active at the time of publication. The publisher is not responsible for Web sites that have changed their addresses or discontinued operation since the date of publication. The publisher will review and update the Web sites upon each reprint.

GLOSSARY

alms Something (as money or food) given freely to relieve the poor.

antifeminist Against equality of the sexes and women's rights and interests.

burka A loose garment covering the entire body and having a veiled opening for the eyes, worn by Muslim women.

celibacy The state of not being married; abstention from sexual intercourse.

chattel An item of property, except real estate; slave.

commemoration The act of calling to remembrance; an occasion marked by some ceremony or observation.

communes Communities characterized by collective ownership and use of property.

conception The process of becoming pregnant involving fertilization or implantation or both.

controversial Of, relating to, or arousing a discussion, marked especially by opposing views.

conventional Formed by a general agreement about basic principles or procedures.

dehumanized Deprived of human qualities, personality, or spirit.

ecology A branch of science concerned with the interrelationship of organisms and their environments.

ethics The discipline dealing with what is good and bad and with moral duty and obligation; a set of moral principles or values.

evangelists People who preach the gospel; specifically, Protestant ministers and laypeople who preach at special services.

extremists People who advocate extreme political measures; radicals.

hierarchy A ruling body of clergy organized into orders or ranks, each subordinate to the one above it.

Holocaust The mass slaughter of European civilians and especially Jews by the Nazis during World War II.

inspired Outstanding or brilliant in a way or to a degree suggestive of divine influence or action.

intrinsically Inwardly; wholly within an organ or part.

karma The force generated by a person's actions, held in Hinduism and Buddhism to perpetuate passage at death from one body or being to another, determining the nature of the person's next existence.

kosher Sanctioned by Jewish law, especially ritually fit for use.

martyred Put to death for adhering to a belief, faith, or profession.

miraculous Of the nature of an extraordinary event manifesting divine intervention in human affairs.

monotheism The doctrine or belief that there is but one God.

oncologist A medical doctor specializing in the study of tumors.

ordination The act or instance of being invested officially (as by the laying on of hands) with ministerial or priestly authority.

paradoxes Principles, beliefs, or doctrines.

patriarchal Of, relating to, or being a social organization marked by the supremacy of the father in the clan or family and where men control a disproportionately large share of power.

Pentecost A Christian feast on the seventh Sunday after Easter commemorating the descent of the Holy Spirit on the apostles.

polygamy Marriage in which a spouse of either sex may have more than one mate at the same time.

reincarnated The soul as reborn into a new human body.

religious orders In Christianity, a group of men or women who live under religious vows. The three vows commonly taken are to relinquish all possessions and personal authority (vows of poverty and obedience) and not to engage in sexual relations (a vow of chastity).

sacramental Of, relating to, or having the character of a Christian rite (as baptism) believed to have been ordained by Christ and that is held to be a means of divine grace or to be a sign or symbol of a spiritual reality.

sanctioned Given effective or authoritative approval or consent to.

sanctity Holiness of life and character; the quality or state of being holy or sacred.

secular Of or relating to the worldly or temporal (earthly life).

sentient Responsive to or conscious of sense impressions; aware.

sexist One who advocates prejudice or discrimination based on sex, especially discrimination against women.

stereotyped Adhered to a standardized mental picture that is held in common by members of a group and that represents an oversimplified opinion, prejudiced attitude, or uncritical judgment.

suffrage The right to vote; also, the exercise of such right.

theology The study of religious faith, practice, and experience; especially, the study of God and of God's relation to the world.

tongues Ecstatic, usually unintelligible utterances accompanying religious excitation.

universal A theological doctrine that all human beings will eventually be saved.

victimization Oppression, hardship, or mistreatment of one; fraud, cheating.

yoga A Hindu theistic philosophy teaching the suppression of all activity of body, mind, and will in order that the self may realize its distinction from them and attain liberation.

INDEX

abortion 19, 21
African American Christianity 55–65
African Methodist Episcopal Church 58
Allebach, Ann 52
Allen, Richard 58, 60
altar service 23
Amish women 45–46, 49-51
Amman, Jacob 48
Anabaptists 46–48, 51
Angelus Temple 32
arranged marriage 103, 105

baptism 47, 50
Bible 23, 27, 29, 30, 31, 33, 37
birth control 19, 21, 25, 38, 49
bishops 16, 25
Book of Mormon 37
Booth, William 31
born again 29, 32
Brethren Christians 46, 47, 52
Briscoe, Jill 33
Buddha 86, 88, 89, 92, 95
Buddhism 57, 87–95

Cannon, Martha Hughes 38–39
Carson & Barnes circus 17, 19
catechism 17, 19
Catholic church 15, 16, 17, 19, 20, 23
Catholics 16, 17, 18, 19, 21, 25, 47, 57
celibacy 17
Charismatics 31
Charm, Tamara 72
Christian music 15
Christianity 16, 92, 98, 103

Church of Jesus Christ of Latter Day Saints 35–43
Church Relief Society 35, 43
community 50–51, 93
Conservative Judaism 72, 74
Covenant Communications 40
cow, as symbolic 97, 99
crucifixion 16

Dalai Lama 94
Deborah 69
Dharma 89–90, 92, 94
Divine Force 111, 112
Donofrio, Beverly 17
The Dwelling Place 19

ecology 113, 114
Queen Esther 69, 70
Evangelical women 27–33

Fisher, Violet 62
Fox, Thomas 21

Gardner, Gerald 110, 111
goddesses 98, 102–103, 111, 113
gospel music 64–65
Gospels 16
Graham, Billy 27, 33
Graham, Ruth Bell 27

"The Hallelujah Gals" 31
Hanks, Maxine 41
Hasidic Jews 67, 68, 74, 75
head coverings 81, 82, 83

Hindus 97–105
the Holocaust 69
homily 23
hooks, bell 93–94
Humanae Vitae 21
Hutterites 51

Islam 77, 78, 79, 80, 84, 92, 103
Israel 69

Jackson, Mahalia 64
Jesus Christ 16, 26, 46, 58,
Judaism 67–75, 79, 92, 103

Kaiser, Grace 49
Kane, Sister Theresa 21
karma 97, 98, 105
Kaylin, Lucy 17
Kelly, Leontine 62
Klal Yisrael 75

Laake, Deborah 40
Lama 87, 89, 91
Lampa, Rachael 15, 25
Lee, Jarena 58, 60
Lee, Linda 62
Lhamo, Jetsunma Ahkon 87, 89
liberation theology 64
Little Sisters of Jesus 17
Lotz, Anne Graham 27, 29

McKenzie, Vashti 57
McPherson, Aimee Semple 31–32
magick 111, 115
Marder, Janet 72
Mary 17, 18
Mecca 80
meditation 89, 90, 92
Mennonite Confession of Faith 52
Mennonites 46, 47–48, 52

Miriam 69, 76
Missionaries 33, 39
Mohammed 77, 80, 84, 85
Mormons 35–43, 79
Moses 69, 71, 75
musical influence 62, 64
Muslim Women's League 81, 82
Muslims 77–85

nonviolence 47–48
nuns 17, 19, 20, 22

Old Order Amish 46, 48
on Priestly Ordination 21, 23
ordination 21
Orthodox Jews 71–72, 73

pastoral administrators 23
Pentecostals 30–31, 57, 64
personal relationship with God 28, 29
Pope John Paul II 15, 21, 23, 25
prayer veil 51
priests 16, 21, 23–25
Protestants 47
Puritans 30

Quran 79, 80, 81, 82, 84

Rabinovitz, Rachel 71–72
Randall, Trisha 39
Reconstructionist Judaism 74
Reform Judaism 72, 75
reincarnation 87, 98
religious orders 17
resurrection 16
revivals 30
Richards, Joanne 77, 79

sacramental rituals 23
saints 24

Salvation Army 31
satanism 111, 113
Seder 75
separation of church and state 47
sexism 16, 84
sexual abuse accusations 23, 25
Shamana, Beverly 62
Simons, Menno 48
slavery 58, 60, 64, 69
Smith, Joseph 37, 38, 41
Smoot, Mary Ellen 35, 43
Snow, Lorenzo 38
Society for Krishna Consciousness 98
Southern Baptist Convention 32–33
speaking in tongues 30, 31
spirituals 64
Starhawk 114
Stoltzfus, Louise 45

Talmud 71, 75
Third Eye 100

Torah 71, 72, 73
Truth, Sojourner, 54, 60, 61
Tubman, Harriet 59, 60

universal church 16

Vatican 23
veils 81, 82

Walker, Alice 93, 94
Wangmo, Yeshe 91
Westwood, Jean 38
Wheatley, Phyllis 58
Wicca and Neopaganism 107–115
Wiccan Rede 114
Willow Creek 33
World Youth Day 15

yoga 100
Young, Brigham 37

PICTURE CREDITS

BIOGRAPHIES

Kenneth McIntosh holds a bachelor's degree in education and a master's degree in theology. He is a freelance writer, living in upstate New York. Formerly, he taught for a decade in a Los Angeles junior high school. He has been involved in various forms of interfaith dialogue for more than ten years, and has also written and spoken on issues of religious faith and women's issues during the same years. He has written ten other titles for Mason Crest publishers, on topics including clergy, American Indians today, Latin American history, and Native Women in America.

Dr. Mary Jo Dudley is the director of Cornell University's Gender and Global Change Department, which focuses on the evolving role of gender around the world. She is also the associate director of Latin American Studies at Cornell.